A FIRESIDE BOOK
Published by Simon & Schuster ■ New York London Toronto Sydney

the joys *of* much *too* much

Go for the Big Life—

the Great Career, the Perfect Guy,

and Everything Else You've Ever Wanted

(Even If You're Afraid You Don't Have What It Takes)

bonnie fuller

FIRESIDE
Rockefeller Center
1230 Avenue of the Americas
New York, NY 10020

For information regarding special discounts for bulk purchases,
please contact Simon & Schuster Special Sales at 1-800-456-6798
or business@simonandschuster.com.

Designed by Jaime Putorti

Manufactured in the United States of America

10 9 8 7 6 5 4 3 2 1

Library of Congress Cataloging-in-Publication Data
Fuller, Bonnie.
   The joys of much too much : go for the big life—the great career,
the perfect guy, and everything else you've ever wanted / Bonnie Fuller.
      p.   cm.
   Includes index.
   1. Women—Psychology. 2. Women—Conduct of life. 3. Self-realization
in women. 4. Success. I. Title.
   HQ1206 .F85 2006
   305.40971—dc22   2005057974

ISBN-13: 978-0-7434-5947-1
ISBN-10   0-7434-5947-4

To the most precious rewards of a full life, my family—
my children, Noah, Sofia, Leilah, and Sasha,
and my husband of twenty-two years, Michael

and to my most dedicated supporter and role model,
my mom, Tanya Warsh

acknowledgments

I'd like to thank the most patient editor of all, Doris Cooper, who persevered through weekly magazine schedules and unforeseen life events and remained committed to this book. Thank you also for your excellent suggestions and thoughtful editing. Thank you also to the enthusiastic and supportive Mark Gompertz, Trish Todd, Cherise Davis, Marcia Burch, and Chris Lloreda at Simon & Schuster.

I am grateful to my agent, Michael Carlisle, who took me on as a first-time author with complete commitment at a very difficult time in my life, and to Bob Bernstein for introducing us and suggesting that Michael get on the case.

I thank you, Pat Mulcahy, for your hard work, willingness to meet and talk between weekly deadlines, and for your total professionalism. You were a wonderful collaborator.

During the time I wrote this book I've had four terrific assistants who all provided encouragement and positive feedback. My thanks to Ingella Ratledge, Jared Shapiro, Kelly Will, and Taryn Adler.

I couldn't have written this book without the many other

women—with lives that are happily much too much—meeting with me and/or sharing their experiences! Thank you, Jane Hess, Lara Shriftman, Stephanie Green, Helen Gurley Brown, Mary Berner, Nancy Haberman, Lisa Dallos, Barbara Corcoran, Amy Sacco, Pamela Wallin, Vaune Davis, Liz Heller, Dana Ardi, Barbara Sgroi, Pat Cook, Bobbi Brown, Karen Duffy, Gloria Feldt, and Donna Kalajian-Lagani.

For many years I had a partner in crime in magazines, Donald Robertson, and together we cooked up many successful ideas. I'd like to thank him for initially helping me cook up the idea for this book and then giving great input all along the way.

Sometimes you never know who will turn out to be your biggest life rafts when you are struggling not to drown. My deepest thanks for providing sturdy rafts—Dr. Rock Positano, David Brown, Keith Mullin, Marcia Worthing, Neal Lenarsky, Adam Baumann, and Dr. David Gottesfeld.

A thank-you to my boss, David Pecker, who has been unfailingly supportive.

Much gratitude to our close "laneway" friends who are *always* there through the ups and the downs: Jenni Stern and Jim Meigs, Edith and Kevin O'Rourke, and Amy Brizer.

Finally, writing about them inside the book simply isn't enough to express the depths of gratitude that I owe them for their genius, expertise, and humanity. So I want to thank them again for their gift of life—Dr. Stephanie Rifkinson, Dr. Michael Weiner, and Dr. Kara Kelly. Michael and I can never thank you enough!

contents

acknowledgments *vii*

introduction
More Is More, Not Less—the Joys of
the Unbalanced Life *xi*

1 Never Face the Facts: The Positive Aspects
of Denial *1*

2 Embrace Your Inner Canadian: How to
Turn Your Negatives into Positives *13*

3 Ignore the Odds: Find Your Passion, and
Go for It! *47*

4   Don't Put Off Real Life: The Joys of
Finding the Love of Your Life and Having
Children   83

5   Check Your Lettuce in the Coatroom:
How to Manage Your Happily Unbalanced
Life   115

6   You Can't Be Great for Everyone:
Sticking to Your Mission   141

7   Eating Humble Pie, Even at the Ritz:
How to Come Back from Personal and
Professional Disaster   169

8   Turn Off the Lite FM: Stay Forward-
Focused, and Wrap Your Arms around
Change   195

index   215

introduction
More Is More, Not Less—the Joys of the Unbalanced Life

When I approach a news-stand, I take stock: after all, I work in the magazine business. The headlines and images that catch my eye on any given day range from the latest celebrity wedding to the newest twist on achieving sexual satisfaction. Sometimes I see an article on someone I admire; I'll stop short to look more closely at a photo of a gorgeous dress, or perhaps I'll pick up a tip-filled, helpful piece for a busy mother.

What doesn't work for me—a mother of four, a wife,

the editorial director of American Media, which owns over twenty publications, some of them magazines like *Star* that have to go to press every single Monday night—are the immaculate, very sparse white covers of some of the newest entries in the magazine field. These are the ones that tell you how to simplify your life.

If only I had time to clean my closets regularly; rotate my wardrobe on a sensible, seasonable basis; cook healthy, organically proper meals every evening for my family; and keep my home and desktop clutter-free.

Even if I had the time, these things would not be my top priorities. I'd rather ride bikes with my kids or crack open a good book. That's much more fun and satisfying than fixating on the forms of perfection shown in the pages of these magazines.

They reflect my idea of a total fantasy realm—and not one that I want to fall into headlong. The world I see pictured in these precisely calibrated, full-color spreads could not be more unreal. This is a world in which no one eats fast food on the run or tries to butt in line at the supermarket checkout because the kids are screaming to get out of there. This is a world in which women can actually talk to their friends on the phone without howling, laughing kids or husbands wreaking havoc in the background. This is also a world, I've noticed, where people have few possessions. They own only three pairs of perfect shoes; read few books, newspapers, or magazines; and apparently open the mail and sort through it every day religiously.

After years of trying to make a living at something I love while raising a family, I've come to the conclusion that a jam-packed, maxed-out, full-to-the-very-top existence is the secret to an insanely happy life, no matter what those odes to "simplicity" say to the contrary.

I've pretty much written off the possibility of ever having peace and quiet in my life.

I guess that somewhere along the line I made the decision that I'd rather lead a life that's a blur than one that's a bore.

I'm not the only woman in America who feels this way. Finding the fun—the joy, the vitality, and the spontaneity—in an overcommitted life that sometimes seems to lurch from one crisis to another is simply a matter of seeing the beauty in all that we cannot really change, even if we're hell-bent on doing so.

▓ The Power in Wanting— and Achieving—More!

In this book, I will share my tips on how to have it all: the career, the kids, the love, and the romance. I intend to show you your life from this new angle, from which you can see that all the things that you think are overwhelming you are in fact a rich, rewarding, and demanding combination of blessings. Even if you've barely ticked off a single thing from your to-do list today, I promise that you will feel good and happy about yourself when you see things my way.

I don't buy the widely accepted belief that women fail when they try to do too much, that they should step back and pare down and focus on the so-called little things, like how to scrub a sink until it sparkles or how to organize the sock drawer to perfection. I can assure you that there isn't one organized sock drawer in my entire house, and I don't give a damn!

Luckily there's no size six body, or genius IQ, or celebrity connections required to live to the fullest. All you need is a positive, can-do attitude and a refusal to drive yourself crazy by letting other people define how you should live your life.

I'm going to show you how to make a road map just for you.

◼ For Every Time There Is a Season: You *Can* Have It All, but Not All at Once

For the time being, I've given up sitting in the park with just a book, gardening for hours, and other such contemplative pursuits, for the joys of having and raising children while building a successful career. Truth is, I've given up a lot of sleep, too. But I'd rather be with my kids now—while they still want to spend time with me—because soon, like all teenagers, they won't. And I've worked hard to get where I am in the magazine industry. Why stop now? I'll have time later to plant irises.

If, God forbid, anything happens to me tomorrow, I

don't think I'll be lying there on my deathbed thinking, "I wish I'd gone on more meditation weekends." I will not lie there and regret that I didn't have more time for *me*. Life is all about choices and priorities.

A noninvolving work life and placid home life will empty your energy reserves faster than any sixty-hour week at the office. We all dream of spending endless days lying on a beach, taking off three months in the summer, or quitting work to redecorate the house. In reality we'd grow bored, not to mention soft around the edges.

Simplifying down to the most precious objects and actions will result in sterility, which is the road to spiritual ruin and mental rigor mortis! I believe in cutting out negative things and people, but why would you want to cut down on stimuli?

I drive my mother nuts because she says that if I have a minute, I'll squeeze five things into it. I always have way too much to do; she thinks that's bad. Yes, sometimes things seem overwhelming, but right now I *want* to squeeze five things into every spare minute. You hope not necessarily for one great moment of victory but for small achievements that add up to a wonderful and fulfilling life.

Ryan Kwanten, one of the stars in the hit show *Summerland*, once talked about how since the age of fifteen—and he's now twenty-seven—he hasn't spent more than four weeks out of work.

"It's been an incredible ride," he says in the article in *Star*, the celebrity newsweekly I oversee.

When the interviewer asks him if he's exhausted, he answers, "Sleeping isn't really a priority in my life—there are so many other things to do. I can catch up with sleep when I retire." I agree.

◼ Plunge into Living!

I'm not the kind of person who yearns to go to an ashram for a week. I think you learn about yourself through experiences—as many of them as you can manage. When you go through the stages of life—when you commit to a relationship, when you have children, when you relate to your friends or work colleagues—that's when you learn about yourself. Few "aha" moments come from sitting in an empty room gazing at your navel.

Most important, I think you gain empathy through experience. One of the reasons I believe I've been successful as a magazine editor is that I can empathize with my readers. Like them, I've agonized. I've been ecstatic, frantic, terrified, lost, exhausted. I know how others feel when they experience those things. I'm lucky, because it's helped make me a richer person.

◼ Don't Play It Safe!

One of the reasons women want life to be "simple" is that the world can indeed be a frightening place: if the focus of your life is avoiding risk, there's little to give you any anxiety, of course. There is also little to excite you. It's like living in some tiny, enclosed space instead of the big, wide, welcoming, sometimes terrifying world out there.

The Chinese once bound women's feet to keep them from getting out into the world—to hobble them. Sometimes I feel there's been a philosophical return to that kind of thinking. Women are hobbling themselves by believing that if they can't do something while being incredibly "nice," or doing it perfectly, or being with the right man, then they shouldn't do it at all. I say, don't wait to enjoy your life fully, whether that means feathering your nest without Mr. Right or setting out on a group trek of the Himalayas.

Stay proactive in all things. Even if the perfect man isn't in your sights, commit to the apartment or the house.

Decorate.

Take fabulous vacations, or go to parties on your own.

Move cross-country, or to Paris.

Adopt a child.

Live your life as fully as possible—*now.* The time clock of life keeps ticking, and we only have one life to fit it all in. There are no second chances, so go for it now.

Learn to enjoy the action that surrounds you every day.

Join me on a search not for the perfectly ordered existence but for the one that makes you happy with its blissful noise. "Keeping it simple" is an impossible task, like rolling a huge boulder up a steep hill, over and over again. Life is a risky, messy business—but a rich one.

Believe me, there is no better recipe for happiness and inner peace than a perpetually jam-packed-to-the-gills life that suits you. Who has time for self-doubt, self-punishment, and self-admonition when you've got too many interesting and loving demands on your time?

Having more also means you'll be giving more: to your family, to your spouse or lover, to your colleagues at work and your other friends and close associates.

More means being generous with yourself as much as you can be, and making others feel good, too. Having a full life will enable you to grow tremendously as a person, and will contribute to a sense of self-satisfaction and a lasting happiness that no short-fix solution like a "spiritual fast" or a session in a psychiatrist's office can ever match.

1 Never Face the Facts: The Positive Aspects of Denial

a few years ago when I was having lunch with David Brown, the Oscar-winning producer of films such as *Jaws* and *Chocolat*, I garnered a bit of wisdom I recognized instantly as right on the money: **"Under no circumstances, face the facts."** David first heard this motivating mantra from the legendary actress Ruth Gordon.

David explained that if he and his producing partner Richard D. Zanuck had read the book *Jaws* more closely and realized they had to create a mechanical shark to make the story work onscreen, they never would have gone near the project. Ignorant, they went forward, and even hired a then-unknown, twenty-nine-year-old director named Steven Spielberg. The rest is movie box office history. *Jaws,* the first of the big summer blockbusters, took in $470 million worldwide, which stood as a record until the release of *Star Wars.*

As soon as the words left his mouth, I realized that, consciously or unconsciously, I had been living my life by David and Ruth's mantra. How else could a geeky, Canadian Jewish girl from a dysfunctional family grow up to be a successful magazine editor in New York City?

If I had ever really "faced the facts" about myself, I never would have reached for even a zillionth of what I've managed to accomplish. In 1989, as editor in chief, I relaunched *YM,* the teen magazine, which went on to great success before eventually folding many years later; three years after that, I created and launched *Marie Claire* in America; three years later, I revamped *Cosmopolitan;* then in 1998 I brought *Glamour* magazine to its highest circulation and profits ever before being very publicly tossed out of the editor in chief position.

Eight months later I landed at the celebrity magazine *Us Weekly,* which I worked hard to turn into a blockbuster success. Now I am editorial director of American Media, whose twenty publications include *Shape, Men's Fitness,* and *Star,* which I have just retooled with the help of a great team, led by Editor in Chief Joe Dolce, from a newsprint tabloid into a glossy magazine.

To make *YM* a success, I had to ignore the fact that *Seventeen* had dominated the teen magazine market for years. If I had really stopped to consider the fact that *Us Weekly* had been written off by the media and advertising world before I was able to revive it, I might have been paralyzed by fear and self-doubt. If I had fixated on the fact that many people thought *Star* was about aliens when I started at the magazine, I would have been in a state of despair from day one. These were my versions of David Brown's mechanical shark.

Imagine a short brunette, with bitten-to-the-quick nails, flyaway hair, adult acne, with no family connections or money, no Ivy League or literary credentials, no appearances on a reality TV show. Imagine her thinking she could land the job of her dreams not once, but over and over again—not to mention find a wonderful man to love, and learn how to keep a pack of personal demons at bay. I've been able to make it happen, and I'll show how *you* can, too.

Adopt a Make-Things-Happen Mind-set

You don't have to be Dr. Freud to come to see that just forging ahead—and not giving yourself excuses for not doing so—can do wonders for your ability to keep unpleasant, unhelpful "facts" about your perceived imperfections in your own personal box marked Do Not Open.

In the Real World, who can sit on a couch each week and overanalyze his or her problems? Staying occupied with truly worthwhile, though often trying tasks, such as child rearing or doing a job you love, wards off self-indulgence and a kind of paralyzing introspection that leads to nothing but further insecurities.

Focus on the things that bring joy into your life: self-obsession rarely does. I'd rather watch my kids perform in the high school musical, make a photo album for my mom, or work with my staff to redesign a magazine than sit on a couch, analyzing my past and my problems. Doing the best job you can, both at work and in your personal life—whether it's dating or raising a family or being involved in your community—is what's satisfying in a deep and lasting way.

I'm sure a therapist would tell me that part of the reason why I work so hard is that doing so distracts me from my inner demons. You know what? That's probably true. But I'd rather take pleasure out of working, and in the other parts of my life. After all, how long can you go on about your rotten childhood, your father's running out on you, and the insecurities brought about by not having the safety net a secure family background provides? How does it help to dwell on these things?

I don't believe in digging down to find out about the roots of the problems. Generally I know where the problems come from; how does further digging help the situation? At a certain point, you have to get on with your life. You have to move on.

■ Silence Your Inner Naysayer

Start telling yourself with 100 percent, rock-solid conviction that you *can* get to where you want to go. It isn't easy. We all have those nagging doubts, those little voices in our heads that tell us, "You're nuts, you'll never even make it close to the top, you're not worthy."

When those evil whisperers burrow inside your head, stop whatever you're doing, and think for a moment: Who is doing this trash talking? A relentlessly critical, unsupportive teacher; an insecure parent, passing on his or her own self-doubts and insecurities; a lover who can't wait to kick you while you're down? A boss or coworker threatened by your work ethic or your talent? Or is it a nagging, negative inner voice?

Start tuning them out, literally. These are voices you know better than to listen to. Every time the negative voices start up, you have to consciously tell yourself, "No-no-no, I'm not listening; I'm going to think about something else," or turn on the TV, or start reading a book, or do some work, or make a phone call.

It's a very deliberate strategy, like stopping smoking. Every time you think about smoking, you have to do something different to keep your mind off it. In this case, the bad habit you have to break is listening to inner negative voices. After a while, they just stop coming as much. Or you stop listening to them. Or you cut them off faster. Listening to them becomes less a part of your life, and they just fade away.

I have yet to meet a completely secure woman. If a woman is beautiful, with all the money in the world and a gorgeous husband, she has doubts about her intellect, or her professional abilities—or what color shoes she should wear to her best friend's wedding. As they used to say on *Saturday Night Live,* "It's always something." You are not the perfect woman—the smartest, the funniest, the most successful, the most loved, the best connected, the most beautiful, the most physically fit, the most fashionable. And neither am I.

If you stop facing these troublesome "facts," it's amazing how quickly they lose their hold over you and stop haunting your dreams at night. Once you lay these little devils to rest, you will have removed the biggest roadblock to getting whatever it is you want out of life.

The biggest hurdles you will ever face are the ones you've built up in your own self-critical mind.

Granted, some people are born into circumstances of poverty or physical disability that present great challenges; others have faced accidents or illnesses that are no fault of their own. But most of us have no such roadblocks in our way. We have our health and our capacities, so take a moment to thank the Lord for these major gifts, and then get going.

If I've managed to shrug off all kinds of hold-you-back ideas, feelings, and people, then you can, too. If I've opened some tightly closed doors and said, "Hey, I'm coming in," why can't you?

It can help to take out a blank piece of white paper and actually list all your so-called faults and deficiencies, the things you use to keep yourself in check. My whining internal voices often said these things:

"You're *not* that talented. There must be a lot of other women who *really* know what they're doing."

"If your ideas are so great, why hasn't someone else thought of them first?"

"*No* great guy is ever going to fall for you: you're not that special."

List these awful thoughts carefully, then put them in the garbage or in a locked box in the back of the closet, which is exactly where they belong.

◼ Don't Be Afraid to Go for the Big Job, the Big Love, the Big Life

If you are ready to grapple with the negative forces within you, you can banish them, like the self-appointed queen of her kingdom getting rid of unruly subjects. Call me crazy, but I do believe there will be a female president in my lifetime. I believe with equal fervor that women across America, and maybe the world, can achieve great things with a little help—some from others but a great deal from themselves.

I can tell you one thing with absolute certainty: there will be no fairy godmother who appears out of nowhere to place you in a job at the top of the organizational chart; no one to hand you a $20 million-a-picture advance of the sort commanded by Julia Roberts. It would be lovely, yes: who hasn't fantasized about such things?

The reality is that you're going to have to go out and *make* happiness and success happen for you against all "factual" odds. Over the long haul real hopes and dreams come true for the women who can differentiate between what many people suppose to be true and what they can actually achieve. Once you've compiled the list of noisome negative "facts" and disposed of it, start making a new one, and put this at the top: **Why Not?**

Say you decide you want to be a pediatric neurosurgeon, so you can save children with brain tumors. For many reasons, including no doubt the number of years required to train in the profession, there happen to be very few female pediatric neurosurgeons. The key to reaching your goal is not necessarily to talk to every expert in the field, many of whom will be discouraging, but to think, "Why not?" and then determine and take the necessary steps.

If someone is going to be the next—or even the first—in a field, why shouldn't it be you? Of course you've got to go through the requisite schooling, but now at least you've given yourself the mental go-ahead, and whether it's because of a deliberate decision, naïveté or both, you're able to block all the nay-saying voices that may be telling you that you *can't* do this. Now you have the energy and focus to concentrate on achieving your goals.

As you'll see in the examples that follow, if I hadn't been ignorant about the obstacles I'd face, I never would have embarked on my own adventures.

Even if you do know about the obstacles, pretend you don't. Don't face facts!

■ Join the "Why Not?" Club

In college I had a hard time silencing my "You can't do it" inner voices. At my alma mater, the University of Toronto, there was a highly professional newspaper on campus, *The Varsity*, which came out three times a week. It wasn't until my junior year that I could even summon the nerve to volunteer to do some reporting for it. Though my goal in life at this point was to become a newspaper reporter, I was not at all sure I was a talented writer; it wasn't until I saw an ad in the paper itself advertising its desperate need for reporters that I finally gave it a shot. If they're that desperate, I thought, maybe even I will have a chance.

At the first meeting I attended, the sports editor sounded the most desperate of all. After volunteering to write for him and receiving positive feedback, I was thrilled to discover that I actually did have an aptitude for writing. I started to take on weekly assignments. Then a man named Doug Bassett, the owner at the time of a string of local newspapers as well as a major Toronto daily, spoke at a career seminar on campus. If any of us were really serious about working as a reporter, he suggested, we should call him for a summer job. He answered his own phone.

Not sure whether he was serious, I gathered up my courage and introduced myself to him after his talk. Then I followed through with a phone call a few weeks later: again, I was thinking, why not? True to his word, he did pick up his phone, and after receiving my resume and a few sample stories, he wound up giving me a real job at the *Markham Economist and Sun,* the local weekly newspaper in a small town about twenty miles outside Toronto. I bought a junk heap of a car and drove myself there every day.

If I had stopped to evaluate the fact that there were about seventy-five equally interested students at Doug Bassett's lecture, many of whom were surely smarter, better-looking, and more talented than I was, I wouldn't be sitting where I am today. Any employer will tell you that the number of people who actually follow up on initial inquiries or expressions of interest in a job is shockingly low.

Score one for the "I can't do it" brigade. It's large enough without having you in its ranks! Join the "Why not?" club, and stay there.

Think of the great achievers who never would have accomplished anything if they had spent too much time thinking about the perfectly sensible reasons why they shouldn't have done something. Why did Ted Turner think we needed another network, CNN, when the Big Three networks served up news just fine? Why did Ben and Jerry think people would buy ice cream with those groovy names, when we already had so many other choices?

Or consider the story of Larry Page and Sergey Brin, the geniuses behind Google, who quit graduate school to start their own company. Their lack of business savvy was a plus. They went live on the Internet, for instance, before hiring a Web master; so while giant competitors like Yahoo were filling their home pages with stock quotes and sports scores, Google had nothing but a search box and a logo at the start. Some people would have been terrified by this lack of bells and whistles. But asking themselves, "Why not?" Page and Brin went ahead in their quest to help people get information as quickly as possible. Now Google sees 200 million searches a day and has entered our vocabulary as a verb. Their focus paid off in creating one of the most successful companies of the dot-com era.

Are there ideas to be explored, resumes to be written, phone calls to be made that could lead you where you want to go? Get on the phone, on e-mail, or to the post office. If you ask, somebody might say, "Yes, come on board." If you ask with enough conviction and frequency, someone will definitely answer in the affirmative sooner or later.

By now you've turned your inner fear into your most potent weapon. You're afraid not to succeed, so you keep trying until you do.

2 Embrace Your Inner Canadian: How to Turn Your Negatives into Positives

■ The Joys of Being Canadian — Really!

It's no accident that Canada produces all the best comedians: Mike Myers, Dan Aykroyd, Jim Carrey, Martin Short, and a host of others. We're accustomed to all the jokes about the vast snowy tundras and the Mounties and our funny accents and our low-key affect. We know how to laugh at ourselves, and we do!

An unremarkable teenager, I grew up in a rambling old

house my parents had snapped up for $47,000 in an old downtown Toronto neighborhood called Rosedale that had seen better days. My parents were planning to renovate what had once been a rooming house that hadn't encountered a new coat of paint in decades. My mother, father, sister, brother, and I moved in from the suburbs, an adventure I enjoyed greatly until I entered the sixth grade at my new school, where I discovered that my good-girl grades and studious ways made me decidedly uncool. I was the geeky girl in the front row with her hand up, waiting to be called on by the teacher.

Coming from outside the city, I had all the wrong clothes: jumpers instead of skirts, saddle shoes instead of loafers, and the ultimate horror hair—a short, stringy, center-parted bob with bowl-cut bangs. My fellow sixth graders knew an easy victim when they saw one. Having come from a place where my next-door neighbor was my best pal and everyone wanted to be the teacher's pet, I was totally unprepared for the pack of mean girls I encountered.

Walking home from school every day, I was trailed by two or three whispering classmates who were close enough behind me so that I could hear their every nasty comment. It was their daily sport.

So I immersed myself in books and magazines. Every day when I finally got home from class, I'd curl up on the couch and read. I may not have had any friends for a while, but at least I could escape for a few hours into the pages of history books, novels, and magazines, especially *Seventeen*, the only

teen *girl* magazine at the time. Ever since my mother had given me a subscription, I lived for the monthly *plonk!* announcing the magazine's arrival in our mailbox.

I read every word on every thick, glossy page, and even pored over the pages and pages of ads. Most glamorous of all, I decided, would be to live life like Katie and Lacey, the daughters of Eileen Ford, the founder of the famous Ford modeling agency, who resided in a townhouse with models in an apartment above the agency. Manhattan was worlds away. My parents had gone there on their honeymoon, but they warned me that now it had become a scary, crime-ridden place.

With sixth grade mercifully behind me, I moved on to a middle school where the other students accepted me more readily. I added *Glamour* and *Mademoiselle* magazines to my list of monthly must-reads.

Fast-forward to my postcollege years, by which time I'd switched my focus from magazines to newspapers. Then I went to law school for a year at the behest of my lawyer father: it was like trying to fit a square peg in a round hole. My major joy in life was running around at night covering events for a suburban bureau of the *Toronto Star* newspaper, then racing back to my student apartment to type up my story and phone it in to a desk editor at the paper (this was all pre-laptop, of course)—all this while juggling my legal studies. Working for a paper that was humming 24/7 was my idea of an exciting job!

When it came time to hunt for a summer job, I applied

to every major newspaper in southern Ontario and landed a position as a reporter for the *Ottawa Citizen* in Canada's national capital. They had interviewed over two hundred applicants for eight slots. The only one who wasn't a journalism major, I stood out and was asked more questions than the others: How did I have time to work for the *Toronto Star* and still go to law school? What were my plans? Being different gave me an advantage, I realized, and I had apparently impressed the recruiters by showing that I could handle long hours, multiple tasks, and plenty of stress.

Later I found out that many of the journalism majors had never even written for a college newspaper or any other publication; they just went to class and did their assignments, which demonstrated little initiative or enthusiasm, qualities that I learned later are highly valued by potential employers.

Overachievers Are Called That for a Reason

If you go over the top on your assignments in order to show what you can do, assuming that you will be judged harshly, you are compensating in a way that inevitably puts you ahead of the pack.

If you're trying to break into a highly competitive situation, do what you need to in order to stand out from the

crowd and to rack up more experience and credentials than your competitors. I was so in love with what I was doing at the *Toronto Star* that working those extra nights was fun for me, not a hardship. I was beginning to see that geekdom had its own rewards, not the least of which was a boost in self-esteem.

Doing my reporting assignments wasn't just exciting: it gave me a feeling of self-confidence and accomplishment. I was treated like a real reporter! I was working for practically peanuts, but who cared? My foot was in the door. I could survive on the salary in the short term. I figured the money would come as I got promoted or moved on to other jobs.

Be Open to Happy Accidents

Once you've worked your way into an opportunity, then you have to be willing to do everything in your power to make things happen. While working as a summer reporter at the *Ottawa Citizen,* for example, I happily volunteered for the 8 P.M. to 4 A.M. shift for six weeks straight, then spent another six weeks writing for the women's lifestyle section. I even braved being photographed wearing a bikini for the section's front-page story about a woman who made custom-fitted swimwear.

At the end of the summer, I was crushed when I wasn't asked to stay on at the paper. For one thing, I had taken off a year from law school to see if I could make it in the world of journalism, my first love, and for another thing, I was broke. Little did I realize then that the bikini story and several others I'd written in Ottawa would lead to a big break later.

When the *Ottawa Citizen* didn't offer me a place on the staff at the end of the summer, I packed my bags into my rattling old jalopy of a Camaro and drove back to Toronto, to the house where my mother still lived after she and my father had divorced. The economy at the time was dismal; unemployment was sky-high, especially for recent grads. Immediately I called all of the assignment editors I'd met while moonlighting at the *Toronto Star* in law school.

I was determined to plug away until I found another job. And if worst came to worst, I was willing to take part-time work, too—anything to get back into the field, even at ground level.

The paper was just about to bump up its fashion coverage, and I was advised by a couple of my contacts that the editor of the Family section was looking for a young fashion reporter. Fashion was not yet a hot area of interest, and there weren't that many reporters around in the field. But I had my bikini story to show her in the interview.

I saw an opportunity, and I honed in. I had never set out to be a fashion reporter: rather, I was willing to turn on a dime and to adjust my game plan, because I wanted a job—any job—and that was the one available.

Here's what I put out of my head: I was never fashionable. In high school, and then in college, I was conservative, dressing in corduroys and scuffed old shoes, home-sewn peasant dresses and clogs. I was an eye roller when it came to the idea of spending money on shoes. I was such an earth girl that I had never even considered wearing high heels: they seemed too hard to walk in. Nothing sexy—I was a bookworm, and a vegetarian.

My confidence in picking the perfect interview ensemble wasn't strong. For my interview I finally decided on a flounced pink skirt; a mannish, short-sleeved white shirt; a thin blue tie left deliberately untied; and blue wedge sandals. I know it wasn't my outfit that landed me the job.

Rather, these words secured the job for me: "You may be able to find someone with more experience, but you will not find someone willing to work harder." Substance won out over style.

In just a matter of weeks, a negative situation became a positive one. I never would have wound up at the *Toronto Star* if the *Ottawa Citizen* had indeed made me an offer. This was a bigger paper, in a much bigger, more sophisticated city, and a more fun beat than I would have ever known to request.

Did it matter that I knew practically nothing about fashion except what I had gleaned from reading my favorite magazines? If I'd fixated on the fact that I didn't have the experience to do the job, I might have been paralyzed. Instead I focused on getting the job. Then I compensated for not knowing anything about fashion: I scrambled to learn, and fast.

■ "The Best Way to Be Noticed Before You're Brilliant at Your Job Is to Do Everything Instantly." — Helen Gurley Brown

Having now overseen seven women's magazines—*Celebrity Living* is the latest—I can tell you that in every place there really are just a few who *really* strive to stand out. In a new job, you don't know enough to be innovative; if all you can do is the job itself, do it fast and well.

Not only did I do everything my editor asked for, I learned to have a sense of urgency.

I have never understood young reporters who wait around to start their assignments. It's important to get that first round of calls out quickly, because you never know how long it will take for people to get back to you, and sometimes they don't. Or they may lead you to even better sources of information.

It is better to overproduce than to come up short, no matter what the assignment.

My mandate at the *Toronto Star* was to produce three features a week for the Thursday fashion section. I always made sure I had an additional story ready just in case we had extra space. Plus I had another tortuous assignment: each week I had to pull together a supercheap outfit from a thrift shop or budget store, then model it for a photo in the meager *Toronto Star* studio. I was hardly model material, and there was no budget for professional hair or makeup helpers. I was on my own week after week on the pages of the lifestyle section, with my photo and a column about my outfit called "All the Rage," looking like a total goofball in the paper.

But I did what I had to, to get the job done. The lessons? Keep a sense of humor, because there is in every job something you won't particularly enjoy. Try to see the bigger picture and don't get mired in annoying details. Don't whine: suck it up and be a pro. Your attitude will be noticed and appreciated by the higher-ups.

Keep Yourself Available, and Book a Flight If You Have To!

I had been at the *Toronto Star* for almost three years when I started to investigate the idea of moving to New York City. My serious boyfriend of four years was a photojournalist who'd been born in New York. He loved his hometown and introduced me to the city, which we visited often. He started talking about landing a job there and interviewed at the hot tabloids, the *New York Post* and the *Daily News*. Though he hadn't yet found work, I was worried that he would move anyway. I was madly in love with him; he was the one for me, whether he realized it yet or not. Determined not to be left behind, I fired off letters to all the magazines and newspapers I could think of in New York. Though my boyfriend provided me with the initial impetus to explore the idea of moving, later I would see that I was ready for a new adventure, a new risk with which to challenge myself.

My first interview in the city was at *Seventeen,* where I was promptly and politely steered out the door.

I had better luck with *Women's Wear Daily,* published five days a week, the bible of the fashion business and an excellent name to put on a resume. Unfortunately my initial query letters and follow-up calls from Canada had gone unanswered. When I finally made it to New York City, after forcing myself to pick up the phone and call yet again, I got a tepid "Come on in to *WWD* if you must."

The funny thing is that once I got into the decidedly unglamorous downtown *WWD* office and settled into the interview with the editor in chief, she didn't care that I was a Canadian without spiffy fashion credentials: it didn't matter. She offered me a job covering knitwear and all the young clothing collections. It turned out that WWD had had a hard time finding experienced fashion reporters. My persistence paid off. They didn't want to be bothered with me—until they had an opening to fill. Once I got in there, they saw I had the skills they needed. I was in the right place at the right time.

I had made my own luck.

Managers are busy. They don't want to scour the earth before they hire somebody, and they don't want to meet applicants until they have a job available. Most companies don't have the time, the manpower, or the energy to look high and low to find the ultimate employee. Once a job is open, usually they're desperate to get it filled because the job is not getting done, or the person vacating the position gave two weeks' notice. Even in a recession, companies don't necessarily have a lineup of the right people for that job.

That's why persistence is important. **You need to keep making yourself available.** And keep growing the skills that will help you get your next opportunity.

With my new job starting the next day, I flew down to New York City on a Sunday night and stayed in my stepfather's apartment. He was in the fashion business in Toronto and kept a pied-à-terre at that time in New York for business trips.

It was 1980, and New York City's crime rate was far, far higher than it is today. When I took the subway to work for the first time the next morning, I was terrified. I wasn't sure what was worse—riding the gloomy, filthy train or walking into what felt like a hostile newsroom. No one smiled, but the editor in chief's assistant, Laurie, did hand me two tokens to get back on the subway to go to appointments in the fabled Seventh Avenue garment district.

In the train station I was so busy looking backwards to see if anyone was coming up behind me that I walked smack into a concrete column, banging my head so hard that I was convinced I had a concussion. Naturally I made a beeline to the nearest phone and called my mother in Canada, bursting into tears at the sound of her voice. She was the voice of reason as she calmed me down. I am grateful that she did not insist I get on the next plane and come home.

At first I was miserable at *WWD*. I went into the lunchroom one day the first week, and a group of women there said no when I asked if I could sit down and join them. They claimed to be talking about a private matter. It was like high school or the movie *Heathers*. I had made the first move, and I was rejected. They were testing me.

Eventually, after a few months, we started talking more. That led to kidding around and sharing information, and suddenly we *were* having lunch every day. These were the people I had to work with, and I decided to swallow my pride and make a real effort to be accepted. Not everybody's perfect, and you have to forgive people for not being terribly friendly when you first arrive. Forgive and forget. Move on.

I'm not a big grudge holder, in general. You have to be selective about your grudges. When people have really treated you badly, and they're incorrigible, and you know they're not going to change—then get out of the way; don't deal with them. But holding grudges saps and isolates you. So save your grudges for the ones who really can't or won't reform. Most people will come around if you give them time.

Just as I was finally getting adjusted to life in New York City after about two years, I broke up with my boyfriend, *who ended up never moving after all*! In my busy new life, I met a man named Michael (more on him later). Always eager to take on more, and desperate to cope with New York's high prices, I'd been writing a monthly column for a Canadian fashion magazine called *Flare*. Through the journalists' grapevine I learned that the editor in chief had quit.

My old friend Jane Hess, who had been a fellow fashion reporter at the *Toronto Star,* passed my name along to the publisher of *Flare* as a candidate for the job. Even though I was only twenty-six and had never even worked at a magazine before, let alone run one, my friend Jane talked me into applying.

The Joys of the Superficial

Once again overcompensating for my lack of experience, I went to the interview with the magazine's publisher, Donna Scott, armed with a million ideas, and wound up landing the editorship. I moved back to Canada with my then-fiancé Michael and was *Flare*'s editor in chief for the next six years. Me, the former hippie girl in clogs, would be attending the runway shows in Paris, in addition to other incredibly glamorous events.

It was at my first European fashion show that it suddenly dawned on me for the very first time that shoes were more than something to walk in. All of the world's top fashion editors were competing with each other in the footwear lineup of the front row. Each editor was wearing the latest, chicest shoes, and each looked sexier than the next.

I finally got it.

The reason that the editors of the European and British magazines were all wearing adorable, sexy shoes, I learned, was that if you want to be a player, if you wanted to stand out, you have to have the right shoes. People give you the once-over. It's fashion: appearance counts!

Substance and persistence got me on the field, but what's on the surface, sad to say, does matter. If I wanted to make this job work for me, I'd have to change on the outside, too.

Don't turn your nose up at this truth: people take in your whole package, eyeballing your appearance as well as your resume before they pass judgment. And don't forget that **the superficial can be fun.** Once I saw that I had to "walk the walk" if I wanted to succeed in this world, I got with the program quickly. I've never complained about "needing" a closetful of fabulous shoes; who would?

So I was editor in chief of a magazine at age twenty-six, but at the time *Flare* had no money. When we covered the collections in Europe twice a year, my fashion director Barbara Sgroi and I were not exactly staying at the Ritz, as the editors from the fabulous Condé Nast magazines like *Vogue* and *Glamour* and *Allure* did. We booked ourselves into pensiones in Milan and fleabag hotels in Paris. In the City of Light, we walked from our low-rent hotel in the red-light district on the Left Bank to the shows—a thirty-minute trek in rubber boots, because it was always raining, and you could never, ever get a cab. The hotel room had pink metallic wallpaper, fluorescent pink bedcovers, and a rug you didn't dare put your bare feet on.

After I got really sick one year, the publisher of *Flare* finally approved an upgrade so that I could get a better hotel. I checked into the cheapest place on the Right Bank and was in heaven. It was only ten minutes from the shows, and it had clean sheets and tasteful wallpaper. Now I had made it, I was sure. Except that I worked for a Canadian magazine: we weren't exactly treated the same way as members of the press from New York or London. Our entry passes to the show tents had no seat or row designations: it was the SRO area at the back for me in my rubber boots, dripping wet. Barb and I would have to stand outside in the pouring rain to even get into the tents where the shows were held, which were packed and steamy and hot. Sometimes I felt like I was going to faint. But we hung in, and we strategized about how to improve our standing at the shows.

It took all kinds of begging and pleading just to get accreditation in the first place. The head of the French show committee, an imperious Frenchwoman, had no interest in accrediting an unknown Canadian from an equally obscure magazine. Persistent begging finally wore her down. Once she finally gave the *Flare* team the OK, I sealed the deal with a giant floral arrangement that cost more than the week at my hotel. But we were in, and I had made an important contact. Barb and I had figured out how the game was played. Once more, persistence won out for me.

Once I got through that impenetrable first door, the door vanished. But there were other, new closed doors that kept appearing in my career. I discovered that no matter how far along you are in the course of your career, you have to deal with them.

In Milan I couldn't even get a hotel room the first year we went: later I learned that you literally had to book six months ahead. Barb Sgroi and I ended up sharing a room in a small pensione. There we were in our twin beds in flannel nighties, side by side, with the bathroom down the hall. Our tickets were for all the shows of up-and-coming designers we'd never heard of, not the top couturiers, such as Armani and Versace. Luckily Barb spoke Italian; she spent the first two days begging and pleading to get us into the big-name designer shows we had actually traveled to attend.

The second year we were thrilled to be booked into a real hotel, only to find that when you turned on the light at night, the cockroaches all went scurrying back into their dark crannies.

We couldn't afford to hire a photographer to accompany us and take photos of all the trend-making looks on the runways of London, Paris, and Milan. And of course this was all before the days of digital cameras and photos posted on the Internet. I found a photographer who was shooting for one of the better-known American publications, and he'd let me go through massive amounts of his film in his hotel room and pick out the few shots that I wanted from each show.

So I spent hours in my so-called spare time looking through his outtakes. Then I carried the film home for safe-keeping myself, in a packed duffel bag that I carried on the plane: I couldn't take the chance that some baggage handler would send my precious parcel to southern Slobovia.

■ Let Your Deficits Get You Over and Up

It was all far from the glamorous jobs and perks of my American counterparts, but I couldn't be in the game unless I figured out how to satisfy a readership that was just beginning to develop an interest in the top fashion runway shows from New York to Paris, and the whole world of high fashion. The coverage of the shows that we published at the time was new and exciting for Canadian readers, and it helped *Flare*'s circulation go up and up.

My next goal was to get better photographers to work for *Flare*. I went on a quest to attract talented young European and American photographers to add to our small pool of Canadian talent. I was competing on the Canadian newsstands with magazines from all over the world, including *Vogue, Glamour, Elle,* and *Harper's Bazaar.* My readers had no innate obligation, after all, to buy a Canadian fashion magazine: it wasn't a nationalist buy. They bought whatever caught their eye. My customers bought the most exciting magazine, no matter where it came from.

I started coming to New York and got some help from people at modeling agencies, who knew all the hot, up-and-coming photographers—the budding Avedons and Irving Penns. I was able to get some of the young talent to work for us but was then criticized when I got back to Canada for using so many non-Canadians. Canadian makeup artists and some photographers were incensed that I had crossed the border instead of supporting our limited pool of native talent.

Reports appeared in the Canadian press about *Flare*'s new policy of recruiting international talent. I was determined to establish that just because *Flare* was Canadian, it didn't have to be small in its range or focus.

My next problem was that the American-based talent needed to see our magazine on the newsstands in New York, but the company that owned *Flare* would not distribute it in the United States. So on one of my trips to the Big Apple, I went to some of the biggest magazine stands and stores and talked to the managers.

I said, "Look, I'm going to send you magazines every month. Just put them out. You don't have to give me any money. Just sell them and keep the money, so that I have some distribution here." Then the models and photographers who worked for us could go to the Rizzoli bookshop, or to some of the big newsstands, and see the magazine on sale in New York.

You do what you have to do. With so few resources to work with at *Flare,* and determined to make it a great magazine, I had to invent my own path. A focus on what I didn't have would have only slowed me down.

Don't Let the Negatives Flatten You

It wasn't until years later, my second or third year editing *Marie Claire,* that I finally made it to the front row at the Paris shows. That brought up other problems, because *Marie Claire's* fashion editors decided I needed a major overhaul if I was going to be on display. A lot of hoopla went into getting me properly attired and accessorized, not to mention polished with professional hair and makeup, because by now television had come onto the scene. Out went the teen magazine editor mini-kilts, boyish, boxy jackets, and vintage ties, and in came racks of black Armani and Dolce & Gabbana suits. I had to go from a cutesy look to that of a sleek, sophisticated fashion director.

Even with my new magazine, *Marie Claire,* and a makeover, it took me two more years or so to get respect at the shows in Europe. If you want to arrive at a great place in your career, where you can express yourself creatively, you can't expect to get there overnight. It takes time. I've taken all the slings and arrows, and stayed in my share of roach hotels, so I know that you can learn not to let negatives flatten you.

■ Keep Your Options Open at All Times and Don't Give Up Forging Connections

After six years as editor in chief at *Flare,* I needed a new challenge. Still in the thrall of the magazines I'd adored as a young reader in Toronto, I felt New York beckoning once again, but it was no easier to get back into the publishing scene there than it had been to break in at *WWD.* Most of the publishing executives that I met with made it clear that they didn't think much of Canadian magazines or my experience there.

And they couldn't pigeonhole me, because as the editor in chief, I was used to coming up with ideas, working on layouts, editing stories, doing promotions, meeting with advertisers, and coming up with marketing ideas. I wasn't just a features editor. I wasn't just a fashion editor. I was used to running my own show. Though I tried to scale back mentally and tell myself, "Okay, I'll just think about feature stories; I'll just think about being a fashion editor; I'll just think about working for somebody else again, and pitch myself as that," there were still no easy takers. Maybe it was my very willingness to even consider backward motion that doomed the effort.

Finally I cold-called editors in chief in New York, thinking, "Well, I'm an editor in chief; I'll invite some of my peers out to lunch." Maybe they'd have a job opening eventually. Maybe they'd give me some advice. When I called the editor in chief of *Mademoiselle,* because it was my favorite magazine, I got back the message that the editor would simply not be available to meet with me—period.

But the editor in chief of *Glamour,* Ruth Whitney, *was* willing have lunch with me. She couldn't have been more charming, and she was very interested in what I was doing. I was bowled over; she was reaching out a hand.

When she called me a month later with a feature editor's job, I thanked her profusely but couldn't imagine myself taking so many steps back. I figured I could take ten steps back, but not twenty. I told her I really appreciated the offer but that the job wasn't the right fit for me. I didn't want to waste her time. I knew I needed a bigger challenge and that it was the right thing to hold out for it. But if I hadn't reached out to her in the first place, I wouldn't have had this offer. Though I didn't take the job, getting the offer was a confidence builder.

It was when I started connecting with some of my peers that things started to click for me. I was viewing them as future colleagues rather than as holders of the key to the magic kingdom.

■ 20 to 1: The Ratio of Nos to Yeses

I kept plowing away, meeting with people. Through contacts, I heard that Elizabeth Crow, the president of Gruner & Jahr, was looking for someone to develop a project. So I wrote her a letter and asked if I could come and meet with her. When her assistant phoned, I took a day off very quickly and flew down to New York to meet with her.

Elizabeth was warm and interested, and it turned out that she had a teen magazine, *Young Miss,* that she wanted to relaunch because it wasn't doing particularly well. She asked me to propose how I would reconceive it. It seemed promising. I flew home, and I went back to work at *Flare,* thinking, "I'll get back to that when I can." By that point I had done so many proposals for various jobs that never panned out, that I had almost given up. I guess I was beaten down. I didn't leap on it because I thought it was another dead end.

A week and a half later I got a phone call from a woman who worked for Elizabeth, Chris Arrington. She asked where my proposal was and said, "You know, you really should get it done, because we liked you the best. You're our top candidate. So please, do it."

I spent the whole next weekend putting together my new proposal for *YM* and sent it out by FedEx on Monday. They called me back down to New York to meet with Elizabeth again, and she offered me the job on the spot.

That was how I learned that you have to keep persisting, because **you're going to get twenty nos before you get a yes.** And when people are ready, when they've got a job, when they've got a need, they're going to make a quick decision.

If nothing pans out for weeks or months, it may not be about you. You may not be doing anything wrong at all.

The right opportunity simply hasn't made its appearance yet. The position with your name on it may still have to be created or vacated. When it is, you'll land the interview. At that point, the person on the other side of the desk can act quickly, because you're just what they need *now*! Looking for a job—or your true love—isn't like batting a good average in baseball. All you need is one home run.

I was editor of *YM* for five years. When I took the job, the magazine was geared to tweens, so I had to grow it up to make it really a teen publication. I wanted to make it more real than *Seventeen,* which seemed to me stodgy and out of touch with real girls' lives at the time.

I wanted to make *YM* warmer, more welcoming, more inclusive, and deal more with issues teen girls faced: how to cope with pressures from friends, from parents, from school, as well as pressures to drink and have sex in order to fit in. I planned a lot of features about guys and relationships and finding yourself. And I wanted to make it more fun. To me, the competition, *Seventeen,* took itself too seriously.

The revamped magazine worked. Readership grew from 700,000 to 1.75 million. In ways I didn't realize at the time, I'd created a magazine for the geeky girl longing to be more than that—the girl I once was. I could identify with my reader, and that made me a better magazine editor. I was providing the kind of advice and sympathy that I'd wanted myself back when my family moved from the suburbs into downtown Toronto.

If I'd always been Little Miss Perfect—the kind of woman who never gets runs in her stockings—would I have been as good an editor, able to anticipate the kinds of things girls and women need help with? I doubt it.

After about four years at *YM,* I had hit the wall in creativity, and I thought that I would never get to edit an adult magazine again. Back then, in the early 1990s, there were a lot fewer magazines, hence a lot fewer opportunities. The editor in chief's job at *Mademoiselle* had opened up, but no one at Condé Nast called me, and I knew it wouldn't be right to call them. It isn't that kind of place.

Then the president of our company, Elizabeth Crow, was let go, which shocked me because I thought she'd done such a good job. Our owner, the German company Bertelsmann, brought in somebody new. Five minutes later it was announced that Elizabeth was the new editor of *Mademoiselle.*

What Goes Down Can Come Up

The funny thing is that what looked like a negative to me then turned out to be a positive in the end. This has happened to me more than once. Yes, I was initially disappointed not to edit *Mademoiselle,* but that missed chance forced me to hang in at *YM* and keep coming up with new ideas. Odds were that another opening would arise, and I wanted *YM* to stay on its rocketship course. Why would anyone consider me for anything if I wasn't doing well where I was? You need to stay open to opportunities that haven't even presented themselves, I told myself. Six months later I heard that the Hearst publishing company wanted to launch a brand-new fashion magazine. It turned out to be *Marie Claire.*

The executive vice president and COO of Hearst, Gil Maurer, whom I had met a few years earlier, recommended me to the new president of Hearst Magazines, and I ended up getting the job.

Instead of focusing on my disappointment that I wasn't called for the *Mademoiselle* job, I concentrated on making *YM* better and improving my circulation numbers, so that when Hearst was ready to start a new venture, my success had put me front and center in their line of vision. **Don't get discouraged or bitter, get busy.** Work at making your goals happen. If the train doesn't stop for you one time, make sure it will the next time.

■ Trust Your Gut Instincts

Recently, when I watched the film *13 Going on 30,* I was astounded by the scene where Jennifer Garner's character, a thirty-year-old senior editor at a *Cosmopolitan*-type magazine called *Poise,* unveils her proposal for a redesign and reinvention of it. She displays for her boss a series of lively, upbeat fashion photos of groups of happy, spirited models wearing bright colors and clearly enjoying life. Garner's character describes how her new version of the magazine will celebrate the power and possibilities of life.

Meanwhile, Garner's former best friend and now back-stabber has other plans for *Poise*. She wants to feature down and dirty, heroin-chic looks that revel in deathly pallor and hints of decadence.

I didn't have two-faced rivals at *YM* or *Marie Claire*, but I identified with Garner's character in the film because I was trying at these two publications to provide an alternative to images and attitudes of the '80s and '90s. People in the magazine industry—fashion photographers, stylists, editors—were in love with what I felt were dark images, featuring ultraskinny, pale, depressed, and energyless models who stared out from the photos with listless eyes. Dressed in clothes that were black, droopy, and sexless, they exuded a deep-seated cynicism and boredom.

I can't tell you how many photographers and models groaned when we described the images we wanted first for *YM* and then for *Marie Claire*—up, alive, active, colorful, and romantic. And we didn't just want solo models, one to a page, but also two models, or groups of guys and girls in couples, often in real-life situations. We were told with disdain that models didn't like to smile, nor did they want to share the page with other models, or jump around, or pretend to be in a couple with a "guy model."

And they certainly didn't want to wear pink. Pink was so out in those days! It was practically boycotted. Models seemed to prefer lying around looking depressed and strung out: this was "art," not our happy, positive pictures that expressed excitement about life.

Donald Robertson, creative director at *YM* and later *Marie Claire,* and I battled what we called the "dark side" for years, and I think one of the reasons that both magazines were so successful was that they expressed a much more engaging view of reality than their competitors. I wanted my readers to feel good about themselves, their fashion options, their relationships, and their looks. To me, the heroin-chic look is about having a narcissistic, empty brain.

We were always unpopular with the in crowd in the magazine world, but our readers were happy. We'd done our job. Lesson learned: **Trust your gut to do what is right for both you and your clients.** Don't worry about what your peers or other self-appointed critics may say.

If you follow the pack, you will never stand apart from it. Risk sticking your neck out if you sincerely believe that what you're doing will delight your constituency. I was confident that teenaged girls and young women want to look pretty and to improve their lives.

There is so much to do in life: we are so lucky to live here and now, with so many choices and opportunities, so much knowledge to take advantage of. There is so much stimulation, and so many ways to find real meaning in our lives. Why would we as editors telegraph to our readers that it is chic to be nineteen years old and already bored silly with all aspects of life?

Donald and I found photographers willing to take our happy photos, ignoring fashion editors who looked down their noses at our insistence on using pink and red and orange in our clothing palettes or having fun accessories that cluttered up what they felt was the purity of their pages. Art directors disdained our desire to use colored typefaces and, horror of horrors, more than one reverential-looking photo on the page.

We were so déclassé. Donald and I joked that we wanted to do a magazine called *Tutti Frutti*, which would be all upbeat and rainbow-colored.

Instinctively, the team at both *YM* and *Marie Claire* realized that women—including young women—need hope and inspiration both on the insides and the covers of their magazines. Hey, I needed these things myself! I needed to edit and read magazines that made *me* feel good. Circulations at these magazines flourished, even if we weren't "in."

Develop an Affirmative Action Program of Your Own: Love Your Inner Loser

You can take everything in your life you've experienced as a negative—your lack of connections, your lack of immense natural talent, your status as a woman about to be dumped by her boyfriend—and channel it toward achievement.

The biggest winners in life are in fact the people with nothing to lose. My inner loser—the insecure little girl who rarely feels worthy and knows she'll have to make her own breaks in all phases of life—has dogged me from day one. She has also motivated me and made me better at what I do. I know there are women who glide through life, impeccable at all times: such behavior just isn't in my DNA, nor is it for most of us. From time immemorial, women have been asking themselves, "How come Helen of Troy always got her eyeliner right, and my forebears never did?".

I've discovered that being born rich, gorgeous, and popular can be a terrible hindrance. If everything in life is handed to you on a fine china platter, you never have that sense of accomplishment, the fulfillment of having achieved so much on your own, against all the odds.

Why You Don't Have to Be Gorgeous to Get Ahead

Brains and personality count way more than being a cover girl beauty. Though these women below always look their best, they are attractive due to a combination of confidence and power:

National Security Advisor **Condoleezza Rice**

Today show host **Ann Curry**

"Funny Girl" **Barbra Streisand**

Former secretary of state **Madeleine Albright**

Pulitzer Prize–winning author and former *Washington Post* editor **Katherine Graham**

Cosmopolitan magazine founder and former "mouse-burger" **Helen Gurley Brown**

New York senator **Hillary Clinton**

By channeling your insecurities into something positive, you can develop a personalized affirmative action program, and you don't even have to be Canadian to try it out!

Asking for assistance is key: I have learned a tremendous amount about how to put an outfit together by asking friends and colleagues who have a better fashion sense for their opinion about what looks good on me. Or I'll find a helpful staff person at one particular store and go back to him or her regularly. Admit you can't know and do it all, and go to others who can lend you a hand.

You need to embrace and learn to love your less-than-perfect inner self because she will wind up being your strongest ally, your motivator to make positive changes, to get ahead in all aspects of your life. And if you never forget where you come from, you'll always be able to identify with a wide range of people. This kind of understanding, money can't buy.

At times life can be a disaster zone: we've all had those days when our period arrives on the day we decide to wear white. And usually we're on our way to an important meeting or an exciting date. I think I've made every mistake in the book. I've stuck my foot in my mouth so many times that it's a wonder I ever got it out. For me this kind of thing comes naturally: my tendency is to a) hope for the best, b) try like crazy *not* to make it happen, and c) pick myself up again after another classic backfire.

Nia (*My Big Fat Greek Wedding*) Vardolos was a full-figured Greek girl from Winnipeg, Manitoba, of all places, who used humor to tell her immigrant story. The multimillionaire cosmetics magnate Bobbi Brown was a short, Jewish girl from a divorced family in New Jersey who wanted to help ordinary women realize their beauty potential. Atoosa Rubenstein, now editor in chief of *Seventeen* magazine, hails from an immigrant Iranian family who fled the revolution there and settled on Long Island. Instead of seeing herself as tall and gawky, a classic outsider, she used her exotic looks and sense of style to her advantage in the magazine world.

Once you channel what you always thought was the loser in you into the world-beater in your field, you'll see the value of taking the negative and transmuting it into gold, like the ancient alchemists, to make the life of your dreams. And you'll discover, as I did, that the former cheerleaders and tormentors in school are rarely the ones who go places as adults. **It's the so-called ugly ducklings that turn into swans, in life as in the storybooks we read as kids.**

There may be days when you wonder if you've been born under a black cloud, when you are convinced that you are overwhelmingly ordinary or that you'll never run your own business or shine in your dream field. Well, let me assure you that there are oodles of successful women with less-than-stellar backgrounds. What they did have was a dream—and a boatload of insecurities that helped propel them to where they are today.

Use Envy as an Instigator

In general, I find envy to be a huge time waster. There is nothing you can do about the fact that someone else may have been born prettier or better connected. Allowing that kind of envy to overwhelm you will simply make you bitter. Then you destroy your own chances of getting ahead, because no one wants to be around a nasty, bitter person.

However, envy can sometimes be a great motivator. If you envy someone else's fabulous house or job, let that motivate you to go back to school or to seek something better for yourself. Use envy as a butt-kick for yourself. Watch what the successful people do, and adapt it for yourself rather than letting anger over what they have—and you don't—hold you back.

Certainly you can admire those who've made it, as I admired the editors of the New York fashion magazines I read as a young woman in Toronto. You have to see the possibilities of the so-called glamorous or more successful life, or you can't imagine who you might become. If you can't envision new prospects, you can't go for them. Sure, it's hard to get going, but you take it a step at a time, like the young women who used to come to New York City and stay in tiny rooms at the Barbizon Hotel for Women. You don't have to start with a fabulous Fifth Avenue apartment.

There's nothing wrong with wanting more for yourself, whether it's a new career, better clothes, a new hair color, a new boyfriend, or a whole new life philosophy. After all, that's the main message of this book! **A life with more is just a lot more fun.**

3 Ignore the Odds: Find Your Passion, and Go for It!

▪ If You Don't Try, You Won't Know

Nothing beats that special, feel-good-about-yourself rush that comes from accomplishment. Some people will tell you the odds are against your realizing your dream: well, what are odds? They're numbers, quantifiable bits of information you can use to convince yourself that something isn't worth doing. Simply getting started in finding your passion, then following it, is a milestone.

Helen Gurley Brown really understood this. I was a fan of her writing years before I worked with her, when I was hired to revamp the magazine as the legendary editor prepared to move to overseeing the international editions of *Cosmo*. One of her signature bits of advice is that when starting out, you've just got to get a job, and if you can't find one in your preferred field, almost any job will do. As she says in her 1982 bestseller, *Having It All,* "Once in the arena, you can begin to grow and to grow up."

She practiced what she preached, starting work at eighteen as a secretary at a radio station, where she earned six dollars a week. She slogged her way through sixteen subsequent secretarial jobs by the time she was twenty-five before a good position came along at an ad agency, where she discovered that she could write well and think creatively. As she describes it, "One job takes you to another and another, and somewhere along the line, your talent—everybody has some—begins to emerge."

Gofer jobs are good too, whether in the movie business or elsewhere. You can learn a lot with jobs like those if you keep your eyes and ears open.

■ Do a Job Well, No Matter What It Is, Then Be Ready for Your Big Chance

Once you get a job, do it to the best of your ability. A strong work ethic is something any employer will notice. It's how I talked my way into my first job as a fashion journalist, when I had little experience in the field. All any interviewer has to hear is that you will **commit 110 percent of your resources to a task, and you are already way ahead of the next applicant.**

And here's another key lesson when it comes to finding your passion: Sometimes you have to let it find you. Some crazy, fluky thing can open doors if you're up for the adventure. **Don't try to box in fate, or you'll miss key opportunities.**

Doing a job to the best of your ability sets the stage for more opportunities. You are networking and laying the groundwork for advancement just by being noticed for your work ethic. Then when an opportunity arises, you'll be ready. This is after all how I moved from *YM* to the job at *Marie Claire.*

Change is always scary, but **you are your own best inner coach.** For instance, mentally map out the challenges that may lie ahead. Then ask yourself, "Is there really anyone who could do it better than I can?" Take inventory of all the things you'd do in the new role.

Don't underestimate how excitement about a new situation can psych you up and help prepare you for what comes next. For example, my association with Donald Robertson, my former creative director at *YM, Marie Claire, Cosmopolitan,* and *Glamour,* began with a casual visit to my *YM* office in New York. I'd just returned to work in the Big Apple after editing *Flare* magazine in Toronto. My phone rang one day and my assistant told me that a Donald Robertson—a talented fashion illustrator who'd done some wonderful work for *Flare* in Canada—was in the lobby. But what was he doing here in New York City?

As we talked in my office in the course of what seemed like a "drop in" visit, it turned out he'd been thinking along the same lines as I had in terms of how the new *YM* should look, sound, and feel. I had a crazy notion: could Donald, a twenty-six-year-old freelancer who'd never even had one full-time job, become a creative director for *YM* and help me realize my vision for the publication?

Over dinner with my husband, Michael, that night Donald and I brainstormed about the needs of teenaged girls and what we felt was missing from the marketplace for them. The longer we talked, the more I realized that Donald and I *had* to work together.

He flew home the next day—a Thursday—and by the following Monday, he was back in New York at the *YM* office. He'd found an apartment to sublet, packed some bags, and turned his life upside down, just like that. Today he is at the Condé Nast magazine publishing company, creative director for *Cargo,* a successful new shopping magazine for men.

None of it would have happened without his willingness—and mine—to act on a hunch, take an opportunity when we saw it, and run with it. He didn't think about how crazy it was to leave his country, his friends, and just show up for a new job and a new life. There were a million reasons not to do it, but he ignored these facts, went against the odds that his move would not work out—and just did it! By the time I got the *YM* job myself, I'd changed cities three times in order to take jobs I wasn't sure I was ready for. If I'd focused on my fears of the unknown in each situation, I never would have moved on at all.

◼ Position Yourself to Be Noticed

You can start out even with so-called small jobs. Sales jobs, for instance, are often disdained but in fact can be tremendously helpful for developing key skills. If you start in sales in a particular field, you will learn how to listen, how to negotiate, and how to sell your ideas, literally.

What seems like a dead-end job may lead to something far more significant if you manage to run into the right people along the way.

My friend Jane Hess once parlayed a part-time job as a coat-check girl in a hotel into a full-time position as an assistant editor at *Toronto Life* magazine. One evening she was reading *Esquire* magazine as she waited for the next customer to check a coat. When she looked up, the gentleman in front of her said, "You know, I used to be one of the editors of that magazine."

Wary that he was joking, she responded that she had a huge collection of *Esquires* at home and would check the masthead. Her jaw dropped later that night when she discovered that her mystery man was in fact a former *Esquire* editor now working as editor in chief of *Toronto Life,* a magazine in her hometown.

When Jane learned that the magazine in question needed a managing editor for its newly launched fashion magazine, she kept after him, checking his coat on a frequent basis, to help her get her foot in the door at the publication. Finally he did, and the rest, as they say, is history. We ended up working together later as fashion reporters at the *Toronto Star.* Then she worked as my fantastic number two at *Flare.*

And you never know when putting yourself in a position to be noticed or discovered or just plain encountered—as Jane was at the coat check—can result in a kick-start to your career, because you never know who's watching. When I was the editor of *YM,* we conducted focus groups on a regular basis. We gathered a dozen or so potential readers of our magazine in a small room, where a hired moderator asked their opinions as we sat unseen in an adjoining room, listening to and watching the proceedings though a one-way mirror. They're like the interrogation sessions you see on television lawyer and police shows, but with the more benign intent of finding out why people buy what they buy and do what they do.

During one particularly lively session with a group of young women in White Plains, New York, I noticed one bright brunette who kept me glued to the mirror with her articulate opinions. I tracked her down and offered her an internship at *YM,* where she worked part-time for two years before heading off to college.

◼ Do What You Love for a Living

Though you don't always have to start at a job in your exact area of interest, your eventual goal is to do what you love for a living. Take the inspiring example of Lara Shriftman, now co-owner of Harrison & Shriftman, a publicity, marketing, and special events company based in New York, Miami, and Los Angeles. As a teenager growing up in Florida, Lara had no idea what kind of career she wanted, but she loved entertaining and throwing parties.

Thanks to her highly organized father, who encouraged her to keep an updated-at-all-times address book, she has the address of every person she's ever invited to an event. But as she made her way through New York University, she never considered the option of party giving as a career; instead she focused on her second love, fashion, and as a sophomore wangled a job in the public relations department of the Perry Ellis clothing company, where she learned about fashion publicity.

One day when her boss was out of the office, Lara fielded a call from an editor at *Women's Wear Daily* who wanted to see some Perry Ellis clothes. Lara seized the moment, hurriedly assembling not just some Ellis samples from the showroom, but whole outfits she accessorized with gloves, shoes, hats, scarves, and jewelry from a last-dash run to Macy's: what she sent over to the *WWD* office were head-to-toe ensembles.

Though she'd never been officially versed in the ways of fashion PR, Lara had noticed that the models in *WWD* always sported appropriate accessories; she figured that the clothes from Ellis would be best presented as part of a total picture. After one of the pieces she sent over to the publication was featured on the cover of *WWD,* her ecstatic boss promptly promoted her to a position as a publicist.

Later, after years of giving highly successful dinner parties with friends at clubs all over New York, she combined her public relations knowledge from the fashion industry and her love of entertaining and started her marketing and events planning firm. She took what came naturally and made it into a profession with the help of skills learned in the marketplace.

To get where you want to go in your chosen field, be prepared to use all the tricks in your bag: a willingness to work harder than anyone else in the room; an openness to chance and unexpected opportunity; the ability to seize that opportunity when it presents itself. Most of all, never forget the fundamental art of being friendly, because you never know when someone you've met in an elevator, reception room, or at a movie screening will give you an essential tip or key recommendation—or appear on the other side of the desk in a job interview.

You Never Know Where People Will Wind Up When You Meet Them

For example, I probably never would have had the opportunity to launch the American version of the French magazine *Marie Claire* if I hadn't had a chance appointment with an up-and-coming designer named Tommy Hilfiger at his showroom while I was working at *Women's Wear Daily*. At the time he was designing an inventive young sportswear collection called 20th Century Survival. We clicked right away, and it didn't hurt that I liked his clothes, too. Soon I was able to feature one of his pieces on the cover, and demand for his line increased exponentially.

After I'd returned to Canada, he went on to design a wildly successful collection of clothing for Coca-Cola. We always stayed in touch, and when I yearned to return to New York, Tommy helped me arrange an introduction to Gil Maurer, chief operating officer of Hearst magazines, through a guy he'd met at the gym who did consulting work for the Hearst Corporation. Gil asked me to meet with Helen Gurley Brown of *Cosmopolitan*.

There was no job available at the time, but in the wake of my meeting with Helen, I sent her one hundred ideas for the magazine, which impressed her. Years later she remembered the girl with the one hundred ideas.

Years passed before my contact with Gil again proved highly valuable when he convinced Claeys Bahrenburg, the then-president of the Hearst magazine division, to consider me for the editorship of an American edition of *Marie Claire* that Hearst wanted to launch.

Little did I know as a young reporter covering emerging designers that a friendship with this young, unknown-at-the-time Tommy Hilfiger, which endures to this day, would lead to so many other incredible connections. **You never know where people will wind up when you meet them.** You don't need friends in high places as much as you have to get out there and connect. As with dating, you will never meet anyone if you don't get off your sofa. And the wider your contacts and range of experiences, the greater the chance you will know what the person on the other side of the desk is looking for when you're trying to get your foot in the door.

So how, exactly, do you get through the door?

I'd like to give you some tips, some of which may seem like simple common sense, yet it's amazing how things that seem so obvious to me after the fact could have previously been so clouded by my self-doubt or nervousness. Forewarned is forearmed. Over the years I've learned, as both an employer and a job seeker, that you can presume nothing, nor can you assume that what you think is obvious appears that way to the rest of the world. It rarely does.

◼ Push Yourself Forward

You will never get anywhere if you don't put yourself front and center with the people who can help you. OK, you've networked even in the elevator, but if you want to impress the big names, you have to find a way to reach them.

They won't take your calls, so don't keep calling. Don't barrage them with e-mails either. Sending regular notes, or examples of your product, is another matter. It's not unseemly! So learn to still the inner voices that may be telling you that such behavior is "crass" or pushy." The "good girl/geek" voice must be silenced. No one but *you* can push *you* forward.

At both *Flare* and *YM,* I mailed an issue of the magazine, with a special letter from me, to contributors and major advertisers and publishing pooh-bahs. At *Flare* I handed out 25,000 copies at the annual Canadian Festival of Fashion. I never considered it beneath me as editor in chief to get out there and promote the product—quite the opposite. Even as you move up the food chain, be ready and willing to do grunt work. At *Star* I am still here at midnight many, many evenings, closing the magazine with my staff.

foot-in-the-door facts

■ **Don't leave long voice mail messages on a potential employer's answering machine.** No person in a position to help you has time to listen to them. If you must leave a voice mail message, state your name and a shorthand version of the purpose of your call. Then leave your number in a slow, clear way. Repeat your phone number one more time before hanging up.

■ **Do write a short, engaging introductory letter** that succinctly introduces you and states clearly why you'd like to arrange a meeting. The letter should be typed, signed, and delivered by mail or hand. Sending an e-mail attachment looks somewhat perfunctory and makes me think that if you haven't spent more time on this, why should I?

■ **Send proof that you are worthy of someone's time.** If you're looking for a writing job, send clips of published stories. If you are applying for a medical fellowship, send published research. Some people just show up at a company, even without a scheduled interview: they drop off a letter and a resume, and even a list of story or business ideas. Don't be afraid of having your ideas stolen. This is shortsighted thinking. You can always come up with new ideas. Besides, most people can't properly execute ideas other than their own. They won't fully understand them the way you will. Even if ideas are stolen, they won't come out the same in someone else's hands, so you're safe.

■ **Follow up with persistent but polite calls** to the assistant of the person you seek to see. Do not be disappointed if you are sent to a key person on staff rather than the person you addressed initially. A willingness to follow the company's chain of command shows you to be a team player from the get-go. And don't be afraid to make cold calls either. Unless someone seems like a stalker, I will sometimes agree to a meeting with a total unknown if he or she has shown talent and initiative.

■ Prepare for the Interview

Once you've impressed the powers that be enough to get an interview, how do you get ready?

Do your research.

Nothing is more off-putting to a potential employer than someone who sounds completely clueless in an interview. Go in knowing all that you can about the company, the product, and the personnel, even if you have to Google the company. If it is a publication, examine the masthead so that you know exactly whom you are meeting with and his or her position in the chain of command. If it's a different kind of company, go to the Web site and look over the list of officers, and read the rest of the Web site, too. I can't wait to hustle a clueless person out of my office, whereas I am glad to answer questions from someone who's done his or her homework. I am open to learning from anyone and will listen to a critical or strongly held opinion if it is an informed one and is presented politely, not hyperaggressively. After all, the people I interview are usually my readers—that is, my customers—so why wouldn't I want to hear from them?

Do bother with your appearance.

Nothing says that you don't give a damn about the job like showing up chewing gum, dressed in running shoes and a rumpled jacket, or with your hair looking like you just rolled out of bed. If you're on a tight budget, splurge on two things: shoes and a good handbag. When people give you the once-over, as I've mentioned before, they always start at the feet. Never wear sheer black hose, which might make you look like you're part-timing for an escort service. Go for the thicker, opaque stuff that doesn't show your skin. On the other hand, if you wear nude hose, keep it sheer.

Above all, wear clothes that enable you to project confidence, which comes from within. Whether your clothes are from the Gap, H&M, or Bloomingdale's, you will be forgiven your style errors—I've made many myself—if you project enthusiasm and positive energy and intelligence. Feeling that you look your best will help you do this. I interviewed at *Flare* in Canada wearing my mother's huge-shouldered, pink tweed fake Chanel jacket—and still landed the position. At *Marie Claire*, I was done up in a very mini plaid kilt, navy tights, and a preppie navy blazer. I still got my foot in the door—and thrived at the magazine!

I'll never forget an interview in which potential executive editor Clare McHugh, now the special projects editor at *InStyle* magazine, wore a voluminous navy and white sailor dress with a bib collar to an interview with me at *Marie Claire*. I knew she was very pregnant, but I didn't expect to see the *Queen Mary* in my office. Nevertheless I was so taken with her enthusiasm, intelligence, and sense of humor that I would have offered her the job of executive editor even if she'd been wearing a potato sack.

> *Show confidence, but of a low-key,*
> *easygoing sort — the best kind.*

Don't show your cleavage, and ditch the strong perfume. A plunging neckline or too-tight clothes are not appropriate for a job interview, no matter what the gender of the prospective employer. And you never know when the party across the desk or the conference room table has an allergy to certain scents. A person with genuine confidence comes across easily and naturally and never strains for effect in his or her manner or appearance.

Don't call excessive attention to yourself.

People who are confident can skip the gimmicks. Avoid dark lipstick and bold polish, as well as distracting hairdos that shout, "Look at me." Think black, gray, white, navy blue, camel, or pastels for your clothes; forget about polka dots, stripes, and any sort of wild patterns, as well as colors such as lime green or bright orange. Anything trampy or trendy is absolutely out.

You can make an inexpensive dress look much classier with a quick trip to the tailor for small nips and tucks if necessary, to give shape to your basic straight skirt or classic jacket. Make sure the hemline is just at the top of your knee: anything shorter won't look professional, while a longer length can look dowdy. Avoid big, clunky, or noisy jewelry, and always wear a watch. There is nothing wrong with a piece of jewelry or some other accessory that marks you as someone with personal style, but don't overdo it. A pair of fake diamond studs cost about twenty dollars and always look classic and pretty. The point is to appear pulled together and ready to undertake any task at a moment's no-tice.

Prepare for all contingencies.

Arrive early to the interview so that you won't look or feel frazzled. Allow time to freshen up your lipstick and hair in the ladies' room if you need to. If the weather is bad and you have to wear boots, bring shoes to change into. Avoid really high heels because tottering into a room doesn't suggest steadiness, literally or otherwise. If you're seeking a job in banking or the legal profession, always wear classic pumps or a closed-toe mule. You can probably get away with a more open-toed look in a creative field such as fashion or entertainment. Hang up your coat and store your excess bags in the waiting room closet so that when you go into the interview room, you have your portfolio under one arm, with the other extended to shake the hand of the person greeting you. Leave the big, slouchy shoulder bag or the teeny-weeny purse at home. Again, tidy and polished in a low-key way is the impression you want to make.

Nail the Interview

Walk into the room like a player.

Don't slouch or slump your shoulders as if you have the weight of the world on them. (You may even want to practice walking or sitting in front of a mirror at home the day before the interview.) Offer a handshake. Germ-obsessed Donald Trump may be dead set against them, but most employers will value a firm handshake. If you have clammy hands, try spraying unscented antiperspirant on them before heading out the door.

Be polite to every person you
encounter along the way.

If you are rude to the receptionist or the assistant to the boss, the boss will hear about it later. Offices are small places. Everyone can be helpful or not, depending on how you treat them. Besides, if you get the job, you will want to cultivate a good relationship with the gatekeeper. You want your messages to be seen and to get returned. If people are rude to any of my thoughtful assistants at American Media, they go down ten notches in my book, because my assistants try so hard to be considerate to everyone. People who work for senior people are almost as important as the bosses themselves. Their opinions are valued; they know the bosses' dilemmas and schedule and personal preferences. They can help you get your foot in the door. Be human with them: compliment them on their child's picture on the desk, or their appearance that day.

Smile at the person you're about to meet.

Look him or her in the eye, and give that firm handshake. Executives meet people all day long and hone their instincts based on this sort of body language. Look observant. Seem genuinely interested; after all, you should be.

Show some chutzpah.

I'm never turned off by a potential employee's opinions or ideas as long as he or she seems to have something to contribute. But don't say something just because you think it makes you sound smart. A friend in book publishing told me a story about a young man, recently graduated from an Ivy League college, who told her that he preferred to read dead authors, because their work has stood the test of time. My friend replied, "They already have publishers. We need some live recruits."

Keep a sense of humor.

It goes a long way toward making a good impression even if you bungle other parts of the interview. If you can laugh your way out of an unexpected situation, you show that you can cope with just about anything.

Keep in mind that you don't have to go to Harvard.

Talent comes in many different shapes and sizes and backgrounds. I heard this first from Gil Maurer, the COO of Hearst, who advised me to be open-minded to new kinds of talent and energy. People—including Gil—gave me a chance when I was coming up in publishing, and I try to do the same for others. When I interview someone, I pay no attention to where he or she went to college. I went to the University of Toronto, an excellent school but little known to those living below the forty-ninth parallel. It's been my experience that some Ivy League graduates can be total duds, and grads of the University of Nowhere can be bright and hardworking.

Exude confidence that you will work harder than anyone else, and voice the firm conviction that this firm is the right one for you.

Even if your degree is not from an Ivy League school, a smart employer will see that you are the right one for the position. My talented former creative director for fourteen years, Donald Robertson, was actually asked to leave the Ontario College of Art because his work was deemed "too commercial." I couldn't have been happier to have him.

Come to the interview armed with ideas.

No one wants to hire someone who is just office furniture: employers want your mind and your talents. The more time-saving, problem-solving, or simply brilliant ideas you bring with you, the better your chances of appearing absolutely indispensable to the employer. If it's a publisher, throw out some article or cover ideas. If it's an ad agency, offer a handful of catchy campaign headlines.

Convey genuine enthusiasm for the position and the
company as well as its product.

This sounds so obvious, but there are people who act as if they are doing you a favor coming to an interview. At the first sign of an economic downturn, the first bodies out the door are going to be those employees who act as if they'd rather be somewhere else all day. I do not hire snobs. Above all, never act bored in the interview, and don't go on too long about yourself. Hunger counts a great deal. Most executives have worked very hard to get where they are, and they are not interested in surrounding them- selves with employees with a sense of entitlement. They've got problems and pressures aplenty and need someone eager to help.

If you really want the position, consider asking
if there's a project or assignment you can do
to convince your interviewer that you are the
one they need to hire.

Nothing impresses me more than offers to make a contri- bution in order to get a job. To paraphrase John F. Kennedy, ask not what your employer can do for you, but what you can do for your employer—or potential em- ployer.

Never start listing all the things you won't do in a job interview.

I have been astounded more than once to sit across from people who drone on about the kind of office they need, the hours they will or will not work, their minimum number of acceptable vacation weeks, and so on. When I hear this, all I can think is that none of this will be a problem, because this person won't be working here anyway!

Be positive.

Never bad-mouth your current employer: it's like a man making nothing but negative comments about his former wife or girlfriend on the first date—what a turnoff! And don't grumble if you're kept waiting. Your huffiness will convey the wrong attitude once you get into the interview room. Never, ever leave if you've been kept waiting, unless it's an emergency. I've been kept waiting myself, many times, for more than an hour or so, but I didn't take it personally. People are busy. If you really want the job, be patient. Believe me, no one takes pleasure in keeping you waiting. Busy people do indeed feel guilty about it but can be overwhelmed by all they have to do, including seeing you.

Promise to be committed if given the job,
not just to work hard.

The interviewer does not want to be going through this process again in six months for the same position. And once you're committed, stay committed. Put in at least a year before asking for a promotion. No doubt you will have to be trained, and the last thing an employer wants once you've been brought up to a certain level of competency is to hear you bellyache about moving on right away. Give back to your employer by letting the company make use of you once you are good at what you are doing.

Don't lie.

You will be found out, sooner or later. Trust is a precious commodity, and once lost, it is almost impossible to regain. Most experienced interviewers can tell a bluff or a fib or a gross exaggeration of qualifications, in any event.

■ Follow Up

No matter how things turn out,
learn to roll with the punches.

Sometimes even if you are great in the interview, you will not get the job. You have to tell yourself that maybe it wasn't meant to be—or at least, not just then. Time and again I've seen people reapply for a second or third time to a company that failed to hire them a few months or a year earlier, and get the job. Circumstances may be different with the company's goals and financial status or with the current personnel. There are a great many factors over which you as an individual have no control whatsoever.

If you're really interested in working at a particular organization, keep abreast of developments there, and try again.

Persistence is always noted and usually rewarded. Even a simple holiday greeting card, for example, can remind the person with whom you interviewed that you're still alive and well out there and that they will hear from you again in the future. Keep in touch, and show long-term thinking as well as real interest in the company. If the organization scores a coup in the marketplace, for instance, send a note of congratulations to your potential employer to let him or her know that you're looking at long-term prospects rather than focusing exclusively on your own current situation.

Finally, once you've got a job offer in hand, don't diddle about accepting it.

If you do need time to consider your options, ask the company for a deadline in order to frame your decision without making them feel that you are hesitating or second-guessing. Be wary of using the offer as a bargaining chip at your current job, because by discussing the offer with your current boss, you're showing your readiness to leave the company. Not to mention that you're risking that you may wind up empty-handed when you put your boss's back to the wall.

If you need to discuss vacation days or start dates or bonuses with the party who's made you an offer, don't allow the discussions to drag on beyond a couple of days. And if you decide to turn down a job, thank the potential employer both in writing and on the phone. Behave with courtesy and professionalism, no matter what the circumstances. Accumulate as much good job karma as possible along the way.

■ On-the-Job Dos and Don'ts

Know that a job is not a right, it's a privilege.

People in the business I'm in complain all the time about morale: things aren't the way they've hoped they would be. They seem to think that it is their boss's role to cheerlead on a daily basis. Some bosses just aren't effusive, or they reserve praise for a job particularly well done—not for mediocrity or a job done begrudgingly. A situation one person complains about might, however, be just the right thing from someone else's perspective. It's best to look for the positives in your work; no doubt they do exist. And if you do need to complain or speak up about something, make sure that you're delivering the goods first.

Avoid the office "black hole."

This is the lair of the chief malcontent on the staff. There's one in every workplace—someone who is seriously unhappy and can't wait to share that unhappiness. This person loves to discuss the "crimes" of his or her bosses or unsupportive colleagues. The slights, the indignities of working in that particular place, constitute the focal point of ongoing and time-consuming conversations.

The door to the black hole is always closed, and it seems magnetically capable, like black holes in the universe, of drawing in those who venture too close. Many can't escape its illicit allure. *Star*'s editor in chief Joe Dolce calls the person who initiates the black hole "a cancer." It may sound harsh, but I think he's right. Once established, a black hole seems to grow tentacles that reach out and suck others in.

I often wonder why someone that unhappy makes no effort to affect change, so that the situation might get better. Such a chronically unhappy employee could also just leave the company and find a place more to his or her liking. Usually such people don't exit until they are forced to, because in truth they enjoy the role they play.

Becoming a malcontent really is the most destructive thing you can do to your career. In the end the boss will find out what's up: bosses have black hole radar and notice which doors are closed. They also notice the drain on staff morale and the lack of productivity. And they resent that they are paying a good salary to someone who spends his or her time backstabbing. The boss will fire the black hole creator as soon as he or she is ready.

In the long run, backbiting doesn't benefit your career, because all you do is make enemies, and enemies have a funny way of *not* disappearing—of coming back to bite you in the backside. You don't want to alienate more people than you will naturally anyway, when you're focused on moving ahead. The world isn't big enough to spend a lot of time backstabbing. Use self-control and don't participate in office gossip, which only feeds on itself.

Don't have an attitude.

If you choose to view things negatively, you'll wind up unhappy *wherever you are.* Attitude is crucial to making the work environment work for you. So much depends on individual viewpoint. Which glasses do you put on in the morning? The rose-tinted ones? Or the dark, gloomy hipster shades that won't allow in any light? You have to ask yourself if things are really, really bad, or do you have unrealistic expectations?

Hang in there.

Once you've been in a position for a year, it's time to review your situation. If an opportunity comes up in the company where you work, and you feel you can do more on the job, or move up to another one, put yourself forward, because in that way you show that you're ambitious, that you want to take on more responsibility. You can also offer to take on more in your current position. Just performing the basics won't get you ahead. It's vital to be mature enough to see beyond your own individual needs, to those of your boss and of the company at large.

Show loyalty to your boss.

I've taken employees with me from company to company over the years because I know they are talented and will perform well. My career progressions have helped theirs as well. Unfortunately, it is also true that in this age of mergers and acquisitions, of downsizing and layoffs, companies are less loyal to employees than they used to be twenty years ago. However, if your boss is good to you, be loyal to him or her in return. Don't forget that he or she will no doubt have to fight for you at some point to get you that raise or promotion you deserve. Pay the boss back by performing.

Make your boss look good!

I have never heard, or seen, this advice given explicitly, yet I believe it is one of the biggest gold nuggets I could give you. If you help enable your boss to exceed his profit expectations, hit sales goals, or beat the competition, you will be beloved and most likely rewarded, big-time. You have to understand that no matter how much the pressure is on your shoulders, it is that much more intense for your boss. He or she has to make budgets and/or meet or exceed expectations for his or her own boss. If you stand in the way by not meeting deadlines, not completing your projects, or not sticking to budgets, you make your boss look bad. And no boss will take that well, believe me.

So enable your boss, and you enable your own career. It never hurts to make your loyalty clear. Tell your boss directly that you are committed to him or her and to meeting his or her goals. This may sound elementary, but you'd be amazed how few people do it.

Here's an inside scoop: bosses have too few people they can trust, yet they *need* a loyal team. If you articulate that you are on board for the long haul, and you then actively proceed to help the boss achieve his or her objectives, you will be appreciated in every way. And rest assured that very few others will make the boss's priorities their true priority.

Learn your boss's routine and make it yours.

I wrote earlier about how routine can help you manage a life that is all too much. Now here's another way that routine can work for you.

Whether you're the boss's assistant or an employee at another level, you can impress your higher-ups by making your boss's routine easier. Let's say your boss gets in at 9:30 and likes her coffee from a certain shop and her newspapers and periodicals available for a quick glance. Well, get in early and make sure all those things are ready and waiting. If your boss doesn't take long lunches, guess what? Neither do you. If he likes memos or reports presented in a certain way, make it your way. It sounds obvious, but a lot of people don't want to be bothered. It's amazing how many times I've watched employees fight a boss's routine, which never helps in getting ahead. If you have a suggestion for how to enhance the routine, make it. Your boss may be thrilled and adopt it immediately. Or your suggestion may fall flat. If that's the case, just move on. But don't let that stop you from making suggestions in other areas of the business. Your boss may very well be receptive to them.

Avoid bad-mouth blogging and other career derailers.

It seems to me that complaining about your boss, or the company where you work, on Internet blogs is plainly a bad idea, as is sending poison e-mail on these topics. With one false click of a Send button, or one acid remark casually inserted into a blog posting, you are making enemies and burning bridges right, left, and center. On the Internet, nothing is private.

Even writing a blog under a pseudonym is not an assurance of anonymity. If you make inflammatory or indiscreet statements, you can bet that someone will call your bluff, even if you are trying to hide behind a moniker. A young woman named Nadine Haobsh found this out the hard way when she was working as an assistant beauty editor at *Ladies Home Journal,* and writing a blog at the same time called "Jolie in NYC," in which she mocked her boss as well as fellow beauty editors in the magazine industry. When she was unmasked, she was promptly fired, and an offer to be a beauty editor at *Seventeen* was withdrawn. Haobsh expressed surprise at this turn of events.

What was she thinking? Negative blogging about your boss and the place you work is a sign of terminal disloyalty and will be treated as such. And just because your blog is not negative in tone doesn't mean that you're home free. If you're employing work time to get it done, or using information gleaned from relationships made on the job, you may also be walking a fine line between what is professionally acceptable and what is not.

Editors of newsweeklies, for instance, do not look positively on editors and reporters who start blogs featuring exclusive reports and gossip gleaned while on assignment for their publication. The magazine is paying the bills and has a right to expect that *all* work done on the job is for that job.

Be a problem solver!

If you want to separate yourself from the rest of the pack, here is one surefire way to do it—be a problem solver. It makes perfect sense: don't you just love friends and family members who actually help you find solutions to your perplexing problems? People like this make you feel calmer and more optimistic. Do you want to add to your boss's problem pile—or help whittle it away? I've had days when every person who walked through my door had a problem he or she expected me to solve, ranging from computer glitches to uncooperative staffers to unmet deadlines. Do I have a sign on my forehead that reads Unloading Zone?

Don't be a needy worker.

Someone who comes to the boss with his or her personal or work problems and plops down and whines and complains and even cries is a burden on the employer. This kind of person is always in a crisis and always unhappy: he or she wants the boss to be a mother or father. Needy workers can never get enough; once you hold their hands through a crisis, they are encouraged to continue this behavior. The neediness will only snowball. Believe me, bosses don't want to be a parent or a shrink. I hate to say it, but women employees expect this coddling much more than men do.

Bosses are, however, usually highly responsive to a true personal crisis, such as spouse's or child's health problems, a sudden death in the family, the diagnosis for the employee of a serious disease. These qualify as real crises. But bad PMS or a fight with your boyfriend do not qualify and should not be shared with your boss.

Learn to be a good listener.

Virtually no one really listens. We think we do, but usually we take in about half of what people say—or we hear what we want to hear. That's why the game broken telephone exists. Listening really well is an invaluable skill that will serve you big-time in many areas of your life. When your boss asks you to do something, listen carefully, and write down what you're being asked to do. Then follow through. You can always read back to the boss what he or she has asked, just to double-check that you've got it.

Follow through thoroughly and quickly.

Half the key to success is doing what your boss actually asked you to do, without forgetting half of it. Listen well, and then follow through. One of my first bosses sat me down one day and explained the importance of listening *actively*. Most people, she said, only listen to the first few words or sentences of what someone says; then they "assume" what the next words will be. But they're usually wrong. She also pointed out that you don't retain what's said *unless* you write it down. So practice the fine art of active listening, and follow up, and you will be worth your weight in gold to your employer.

Do every task to the best of your ability.

Your boss will notice if you're doing work above and beyond the call of duty. You could be a junior editorial assistant and stand out, and you could be somebody with a senior job and stand out. Wherever you are, believe me, you'll get noticed if you listen to what your boss wants, and you deliver it! If your boss wants you to write up a certain report every day and has asked you to have it done by noon, have it done by noon—or by 11:30 A.M.—every day. Be consistent.

What many workers don't realize is that even if you're doing something that you think is a small thing, it's important. Don't make that judgment that it's small. You are providing a valuable service to your bosses—never a small thing, believe me. You have to try to understand the value of what you're being asked to do. If you don't understand why your boss needs you to do something, ask—but in a positive way: "Maybe I could think of a better way to do it, or I could do even more for you if I understand what your need is." Most people, unfortunately, if they don't understand why they're doing a task, will whine or just stop doing it or be unenthusiastic—or bring it in as if they're doing the boss a big favor. That is not the way to be a star or to succeed. If you do even small things well, you get more responsibility.

Always go above and beyond.

Say your boss tells you, "I need X, Y, and Z." If you understand what he or she is looking for, you may say, "I bet if I came up with W on top of it, that would be even better." It would! Volunteer to help out. Maybe the company is planning an event, a seminar. Whatever it is you do, sometimes volunteer to take on more. Bring in an extra client. Call on a connection of some sort so that you can impress.

Don't get stuck, if you're in a field that just isn't right for you.

You have to be open-minded about taking steps backward if you aren't happy where you are and want to start over. If you're miserable in a job, you're not going to move forward in that field. I know women who went all the way through law school and then practiced law, all the while hating it. They just kept thinking things would get better, so they stuck it out. People do the same thing with relationships. If you are miserable, make the change. Make a cutoff point for yourself, and if the job still isn't working, give yourself permission to try new opportunities.

Think about a second career.

There's no reason you can't take a passion you've always regarded as a hobby or an avocation and turn it into a second career as your life changes and evolves. My dream alternative career would be to work at a plant nursery: I love gardening and could patrol my garden all day long—if I didn't have four kids to chase or a job to do. I would like to learn everything I could about the business. Who knows? One day . . . Have as many passions and interests as possible, and you will have more options as your life progresses.

4 Don't Put Off Real Life: The Joys of Finding the Love of Your Life and Having Children

by now you may be wondering: Is Bonnie Fuller all about career? Where did she fit in the husband, not to mention the four children? Isn't this book about having the most inclusive—if untidy—life possible?

Yes, it is. And every day you see another magazine article, or feature on a TV newsmagazine show, questioning the wisdom of women trying to have the whole enchilada:

career, love life, and children. Many women who were formerly career-driven call it quits once children come into their lives.

Guilt and exhaustion can become overwhelming; staying home with the kids, seeking a "simpler," "more balanced" life, seems like a saner option. But what if you love your career, even if combining it with a husband and kids is a huge juggling act?

And let's be realistic. What about the vast majority of women—myself included—who cannot afford to drop out and just raise the kids? In my family I am the main breadwinner. Today most families desperately need two paychecks.

■ Having the Whole Enchilada

I knew I would always work, even if I didn't have any children, or even a husband, but I truly believe that **the most fulfilling path in life involves discovering your passion, then finding the career that allows you to express that passion, then layering in love and family.**

As my friend and fellow journalist Pamela Wallin said when appointed consul general of Canada in 2002, **"A job doesn't give you a career, it gives you a life."** She was quoting Henry Ford, and I'm with both of them. The fact is that the more you accomplish in life, the better you'll feel about yourself, and once you like yourself, you'll be more likely to find the love of your life. There is no need to see your career and a life outside it as two separate and unrelated entities. The stimulating career will inevitably make your personal life more interesting.

When we're engaged in our work, we're more dimensional, hence more interesting and appealing. We like ourselves better, and others do, too. When we're fulfilling our passion, we radiate confidence, something to which men are irresistibly drawn. Most importantly, a fulfilled, self-confident woman will not settle for a man who doesn't treat her with the love and appreciation she deserves. If she sees herself as someone who is accomplished and lovable, and on a unique mission, she won't obsess about her imperfections.

Instead she'll feel confident that she is fully worthy of the right man's love and devotion when he enters her life. **The right man is one who will totally respect you and allow you to be you. He won't try to change or control you, or demean you.**

◼ If You Sideline Your Career and Stay Home with the Kids, Where Will You Be If, God Forbid, Things Go Haywire?

Let's not forget about the money. A paycheck gives you something in your love relationships that may not be wildly romantic, but it is essential—independence.

Depending on a man financially was a nearly devastating problem for my mother, and for many women of her generation. My father left my mother just weeks after my parents' twentieth wedding anniversary. It was the day after my brother Steven's bar mitzvah, and the day of my eighteenth birthday.

They'd been married when my father was twenty-four and my mother nineteen. A law student, Dad drove a cab after school and on weekends to support himself and his young wife. His father ran a not-so-prosperous delicatessen in downtown Toronto, so Dad had to make it on his own.

To make a contribution—and because she loved the job—Mom worked as an elementary school teacher. She'd gone to Teacher's College against the wishes of her own father, who didn't believe that women should work. But when she became pregnant with me unexpectedly, the principal of the school asked her to leave. She loved her job and fought to keep it, bravely refusing to quit because it was "unseemly" for her students to see a pregnant woman standing in front of the classroom. The principal kept pressuring her, but she refused to leave until she was ready— shortly before I was born.

My mother would have continued to work if she could have, but after I arrived, she stayed home, because my parents couldn't afford a babysitter.

Apparently I was a very colicky child, and my father had to study in the lobby of our apartment building or sit out on the postage-stamp-sized balcony, since I was always crying. Eventually he graduated and set up an increasingly successful practice in real estate law. Two and a half years after I was born, along came my sister, Judy, followed by Steven.

By the time I hit adolescence, my parents' marriage was in serious trouble. When my father started spending more and more nights "working late" at the office, his arguments with my mother grew more heated and frequent, and the tension at home became unbearable.

Still, his departure was a shock. And there was worse to come: when he left us, it wasn't just an emotional loss but also a huge financial readjustment. Suddenly mortgage payments were missed, electric bills lapsed, and the heat was turned off because the bills hadn't been paid. Then one day the sheriff showed up at the door with legal papers threatening to repossess the house because the taxes on the property hadn't been paid either. While my brother and sister and I had not grown up in the lap of luxury, we had felt protected and secure. Now we had no money: my college tuition was in jeopardy, and more than once I was officially "disowned" for disagreeing with what my father was doing.

My mother felt lost. Not only was she coping with living alone for the first time in her life, but she also had three kids to raise and no means of support. She confided that she wished she had never given up her career and allowed herself to become so emotionally and financially dependent on anybody. And I couldn't help but feel that she was right. To survive, she studied for her real estate license and worked successfully as an agent for some time. Eventually she updated her teaching credentials and worked as a substitute teacher, but things were never the same.

■ You Need to Prepare for All Contingencies

Thirty years later there are still many women who would be financially and emotionally wiped out by a divorce. Given what I've experienced, even a strong, solid marriage can't erase a trace of inbred caution, a need to know that even if my children and I were left in the lurch, we wouldn't fall apart. My father's leaving forced me to face the fact that I wasn't going to work just because I liked my job, but also because I needed to make a living. Few of us have a fallback position, a safe house to return to if life doesn't pan out. Finding a man to share your life with is a totally wonderful and worthy ideal, but the mental and monetary rewards of building a real career for yourself are priceless.

■ "Must Have" Lists, "Won't Do" Lists, and Other Futile Notions

Many of the women working for me in their mid and late thirties aren't married, and I wonder if they ever will be, given that they expect to meet Mr. Perfect. They have a long checklist of what he has to have: he has to be handsome, and taller than they are, and in a certain age bracket. Most important, he has to have earning power: a job on Wall Street is preferred. Maybe these women are secretly hoping to stop working and be supported; maybe they think they can't respect someone who doesn't earn more than they do. Maybe it's part of wanting to "marry up."

They remind me of my friends who paralyze themselves with what I call "won't do" lists:

"I won't get an apartment or buy a house until I meet the right guy and I'm ready to settle down."

"I won't bother redecorating. What's the point, because when I get married, I'll have to redo it all anyway."

These women are living not a full life but a confined one, defined by negatives instead of positives. Even if your goal is a great job and a great man, the point is not to stall in one area in order to find the other. **Go for broke in all areas of your life. Don't wait for Mr. Totally Perfect, and things will fall into place in a way that will amaze you.** Throw away those "won't do" lists today!

Work Won't Get in the Way of Love

I have friends, colleagues, and staff members who have rightly raised this issue: if you love your work, and work long hours, will you ever find a man—that is, the *right* man?

If you commit to a job wholeheartedly, will you ruin your chances of ever finding someone to share your life with? Recently, a thirty-four-year-old friend who is gorgeous and talented and has received regular promotions where she works wondered if her job was standing in the way of finding a husband. She pointed out to me that I was lucky to find my husband, Michael, before my work commitments became as intense as they are today.

I don't believe that commitment to your passion ever truly stands in the way of fulfillment in other areas of your life. You're not at work every minute of the day.

I still think it's the mental "must have" lists that keep people from seeing a potential mate. I told my friend that she has some tough "must haves" on her list and that maybe she needs to cross off some of those requirements. She needs to focus on men who really appreciate who she is; she needs a man to love all of her, and not someone who will ask her to forgo her ambitions.

Instead she is worried that her job commitments will turn off a man who needs her to be at *his* side and support him all the time. I wonder if she's using work as a shield to avoid taking the risks involved in a real relationship. Maybe she needs to take a long look in the mirror and address her fears forthrightly.

■ Say Yes Only to Unconditional Love

Above all, you can commit only to a man who loves you wholeheartedly, which means unconditionally. You can't marry a man who loves you for your looks or your status, and you can't marry a man because of the fabulous lifestyle he provides. You need someone who will be your partner in dealing with all the ups and downs, the humps and hurdles that come along. It's only with your partner's unconditional love that you'll be able to tough out the challenges ahead.

I've been married now for over twenty-two years: I was

engaged after dating for only four months. I didn't know my husband, Michael, was "the one" on the first date. I did enjoy our first date, though it wasn't fancy. He wound up tagging along with me to the YMHA on a Sunday morning, and after we did a swim workout, I made him French toast at my place, and we went out for a walk. Date two was dinner at a Mexican restaurant, where we split the bill because I knew Michael, still an architecture student, didn't have a lot of money. On date three he cooked me a wonderful dinner, and I was introduced to the fact that he is an amazing cook. I've met women with a $100 first date minimum; if he doesn't spend that much the first time out, he's history. Puleeze! You won't find love with that attitude.

There's something to be said for not going strictly with first impressions. A lot of women think that if a guy, or another woman, doesn't make a great first impression on them, or that if they don't *really* like this new person, they should write him or her off. I think women act this way more in romantic relationships than anything else, but they do it with potential friends, too. If it's not an insta-get, they don't pursue it. They don't stay open to it. That's a mistake.

If you don't stay open to the widest range of people and experiences possible in your life, you are limiting yourself. You can't achieve the full life overnight, and sometimes relationships with staying power ignite more slowly. It's not always the "love at first sight" scenario so beloved by Hollywood films.

There are also great people you meet to whom you're instantly attracted, romantically, and whom you instantly want to befriend. The moment I met my friend Donald, I was attracted to him. He's still a really close friend. Ditto for my best friend, Jane Hess. But there are other people in my life I didn't particularly fall for immediately, who did become good friends in time. Chemistry can develop.

The first time I met Michael, it was at a party thrown by a mutual friend from Toronto. I didn't look at him and say to myself, "Wow, he's really cute; I really want to know him." I didn't. However, when I actually started talking to him about our shared Canadian roots an hour or so later, I realized how appealing he was. He was fun, and he became more and more attractive to me. But I certainly wasn't in love with him by the end of the evening. There have been other men I've met who did wow me right away, but I'm not married to them.

A strong initial mutual attraction doesn't always translate into something long-term. You can't rely only on your first impression, or even a second impression. In the *New York Times* you read all kinds of stories in the "Vows" column, which reports on a particular wedding each week. The column always describes how the couple met. It's amazing how many of the stories are about people who were friends for a long time before the chemistry kicked in, or who met each other several times before they hit it off. Relying on immediate judgments can limit you.

■ Ultimatums and Other Permissible Strategies

On our third date, I laid it on the line with Michael: I told him I was not going to spend another six years waiting for someone else to make up his mind, as I had with my last boyfriend, the fellow journalist who'd brought me to New York in the first place. I'd been madly in love with him, but he wouldn't commit, even after all those years of dating. I was not about to make the same mistake twice.

I wanted to get married and have kids. I told Michael he had a six-month deadline: if we were in love after six months together, he had to be ready for The Big Commitment, or the relationship was over. Instead of being shocked or offended by my forthrightness, Michael thought it was hilarious.

The ultimatum presented him with a challenge: no one had ever said anything like this to him before. **If you want to get married, and you meet the right man and he isn't getting down to it, an ultimatum is completely acceptable.** There's nothing like a deadline to help a man make up his mind, though of course you can't drag him to the altar. He has to want to go. The fact that my forthrightness didn't turn off my future husband helped me realize that he was the right one for me.

Pieces of my life were starting to fall into place.

Michael proposed after four months, two months ahead of the deadline! Show some of the same determination and self-respect in your personal life that you do in the office, and you'll see results.

I talk to young women all the time with boyfriends who have commitment issues. The boyfriend of one young woman I know even bought an engagement ring but then wouldn't set a wedding date, and he only bought the ring after the woman moved out when he wouldn't commit after two years of their living together. Yet after moving out, she is still seeing him; she can't just cut him off.

She claims to be madly in love with him and wants to keep giving him more chances to make things right. In fact what she's really doing is delaying her own chances for happiness. For some reason this man isn't sure enough about her to commit firmly. Or maybe he's a dyed-in-the-wool commitment-phobe. In either case, she needs to move on.

If a man keeps putting you off, and you let him, you are just preparing yourself for more pain in the long run by ignoring or denying the noncommitment issue in the short term.

I firmly believe that you have more than one potential true love. My husband may cringe to hear me say this, but given that I went through a situation where I was crazily in love with someone for six years and thought that was "it" for life, then broke up with him and met my husband two months later, I know you can fall deeply in love more than once. And if I hadn't had the nerve to cut it off with Mr. Can't Commit, I wouldn't have been in a position to meet the future father of my children.

It's a big world out there, with many opportunities. And you can fall in love with different aspects of people. You don't have to "settle." You can take a stand on the truly important qualities in a person and wait until you find them. And you *can* move on. A broken heart *will* mend in time.

After I broke up with my long-term boyfriend, I kept busy. Wherever you live, there are always things you can do to get back out there and keep your options alive: I know this sounds predictable, but it happens to be true. There are cultural events, cooking schools, art schools—not to mention Internet dating. You can get a dog and walk it in a busy park where men work out. Just get up off your couch and get out of your apartment or your house.

I have a friend who went through both breast cancer and the difficulties of divorce at age thirty-seven. It was the cancer that made her realize that she and her husband had grown apart. Finally she separated, and there she was in the suburbs, with two kids. You would think she'd have a hard time meeting guys. She joined a hiking club and on weekends she was out meeting people.

She started dating and using an Internet dating service. The first guy she met on the net turned out to be her future husband. He'd written in his profile that he only wanted a woman who lived in New York City. Now he's moved to a suburb of the city and they've happily melded their families. The point is that my friend did not sit at home bemoaning her fate. Taking the initiative to join the hiking club helped her gain the self-confidence that made her an attractive date.

Even with a busy work schedule, you can find time to go to parties and events, to be introduced to people by friends, to go to a workout or play tennis. You have to carve out the time and make it a priority. And in truth I think we work harder and more efficiently when we are pressed for time. Keep your life full and multidimensional, and you can work and play hard in equally enjoyable measure.

■ There's Never a Right Time to Have a Baby

So what happens after you find a committed love?

You start to think—kids.

I never considered myself a particularly maternal person. As a teenager, I hardly ever babysat my younger sister and brother or coddled the other kids on the block. So take it from an improbable mother of four: when the kids come along, you will love them. You can't help yourself! And they will help you live life to the fullest in ways you never dreamt possible.

When the doctor handed me my firstborn, Noah, I had no idea what to do with him. Naturally I handed him to my husband, who wasn't any more clued in than I was. He immediately put Noah back in his newborn bassinet.

Things were no better when we got home from the hospital. After we walked into our little house with the new bundle, I sat down on the narrow steps leading up to the second floor, with Noah in my arms, and promptly burst into tears. I didn't know *what* to do. Noah, of course, survived, as Michael and I learned the basics of baby care: what we didn't know didn't kill Noah, or ourselves. We adjusted our routine to accommodate the newest member of the household. We learned, and quickly.

If I hadn't become pregnant the first time by accident, I'm sure I would have been one of those women who put things off, waiting for the "perfect time" to start a family. But here's what I've learned: having a baby upsets your perfectly ordered applecart in the happiest way possible. Adding a child to an already busy life is like putting a carton of eggs on top of a full cart, in which everything is about to either fall off the top or crash through the bottom. But once you make it home, you can make a delicious omelet from those scrambled eggs.

Biology Waits for No Woman

In trying to start a family, as in looking for your life's work, real success involves not only making a concerted effort over a sustained period of time, but also acknowledging that there are some things you just can't control. For a woman, fertility is certainly one of them.

Obviously it makes sense to try to have children at the most fertile time in your life, your early twenties and into your thirties. But for many of us, that isn't possible. Still, one of the most important lessons I would pass on to the next generation is **heed your biological clock.** Try not to wait until your late thirties or early forties to start having children if you really want them. **Hunt for a man as hard as you would for a job, if having children is a top priority for you.**

Of course it is tempting to put off having a baby. A career is important to you. Finding the right guy is hideously hard. You're under stress and already feel you have too little time for yourself. You want to take that dream vacation in Tuscany. I understand all that. But believe me when I tell you that there is nothing worse than being hit with big waves of baby lust just when you can't get pregnant, no matter how hard you try.

I see so many young working women who put off having a family for fear of falling "off track" in their careers, or for fear that they can't manage it all. There's no question that it is a struggle. You see her as a caricature in the media: the modern mother as a hydra-headed multitasker, with a cell phone in one hand and the handle of a baby carriage in the other. The woman who works—for financial or other reasons—and still chooses to be a mother remains an object of guilt-inducing ridicule, suspicion, and unwelcome projection of other people's issues.

But the bottom line is that children are worth making an already busy life truly nuts, for reasons you might never have anticipated:

1. **Having kids with the right man will bond you together as a couple in wonderful and surprising ways.** What with the child-birthing, the baby's all-night crying jags, the emergency visits to the hospital, the ballet recitals, and the parent-teacher conferences, you two are hanging in there together, sharing the full life's challenges as well as its rewards. No one else but your fellow parent will ever love and care for your children as you do. And your relationship will be the stronger for it.

2. **Having children puts life into perspective.** You can't focus solely on climbing the ladder at the office, or having a bad hair day, when you have to get home to make dinner and snuggle and cuddle with a little person who needs you to read him or her a bed-time story. It is certainly more fun than eating Chinese at your desk every night until ten, as I was in danger of doing.

3. **Children bring you into your local community.** Having kids gives you a stake in making the world a better place, whether it involves improving the schools or creating a world you want to hand over to the next generation.

4. **Despite all the tears and headaches, children are a lot of fun.** Babies start smiling at about six weeks and laughing a few weeks later. I still smile when I think back to my son Noah's fixation on costumes from ages three to five. For two years, he rarely wore clothes, preferring to dress exclusively in superhero pajamas: Ninja Turtles, Spider-Man, Peter Pan, and Superman. He wore a cape and a fake sword every day. My youngest, four-year old Sasha, recently asked me where the moon's mommy is—good question! He makes me see the world in a new and different light.

5. **Having children helps you discover previously hidden resources within yourself.** You discover many new things about yourself, including a selflessness you have to have as a parent. Most parents put their kids first and bend over backward to do what they think is right for their children. They make sacrifices for their children all the time. As a parent, you have to move beyond your fixations on personal emotional issues and anxieties. You can't just sit and self-absorb: personal growth comes from what you accomplish in the outward world and what you do for other people. Bringing a smile to a kid's face is satisfying in a way that just sitting and contemplating your problems will never be. Whatever you give to others comes back to giving to you, as well. Having children—creating your own family—is the culmination of this principle.

Once you have kids, you can't imagine not having them in your life. Have you ever met a mother who said, "I wish I'd never had kids?" Enough said.

At age thirty-eight, with two beautiful children ages eight and four, I was once again consumed by baby lust. Michael and I decided we would try again. But after three months, I still wasn't pregnant. Though my doctors weren't worried—three months is hardly a long time—intuitively I knew there was a problem, because I had conceived so easily in my previous pregnancies.

It turned out that I was right. Who knew that after years of bicycle riding, Michael had developed something called varicoceles: varicose veins in a man's key areas? Having these veins warm the sperm-producing machinery too much affects sperm production. Subsequent in vitro fertilization treatments followed, but we were devastated to discover that I was one of those rare women whose eggs respond badly to fertility drugs.

Months and then years passed, but I refused to give up hope. Michael had a special procedure designed to help men in his situation. The wonderful doctors at NYU Medical Center (particular thanks to Dr. Nicole Noyes) helped me trace my ovulation to the right moment and encouraged us to keep trying the old-fashioned way, because you never know.

Despite the fact that my official chances of getting pregnant without in vitro still weren't exactly great, miracle of miracles, along came our daughter Leilah. Three years later, insane woman that I am, I tried again, with the help of the clinic, to track my ovulation. Despite even greater odds given my increased age, I had a fourth child, our son Sasha.

Contrary to the gloomy statistics I've read in news magazines—those odds again—I have found that most of the women I know who've participated in fertility treatments eventually had a baby.

Big Family Living

Many people ask me why I have four kids, as though it's some sort of aberration. Once the older two started growing up, I got baby lust, pure and simple. We so enjoyed having a little one again: it was such a pleasure for both my husband and me, and for the two older children.

Then I started thinking about the six-year gap between the older two and the baby, how she'd be alone once they were out of the house at college. I reasoned that Leilah needed someone to keep her company. Each new child brings such joy and new experiences to the rest of us.

I have to admit also that the trauma of almost losing a child probably made us value the importance of having a family more than ever. We almost lost my older daughter, Sofia, now fourteen, to a brain tumor when she was three. The experience made me and Michael even closer and more ready to expand our family. When our third child, Leilah, was diagnosed with acute lymphoblastic leukemia when she was five, it was wonderful that she had her little brother, Sasha, then two, who proved to be such a comfort to her when she was ill. For most of the first year of her treatments, Leilah was so sick that all she could do many days was lie on the couch. She could barely raise her head. Having this little guy jabbering away, keeping her company, playing around her, lifted her spirits. What's more, Leilah was so sick that all she could do with her friends when they came to visit was watch a movie with them. The friends would then get restless, which made her feel inadequate. Sasha, however, never tired of her company, even if she couldn't fully participate in the fun. She was too ill to play but watched her brother do so at her side. His being there helped her get well, I am sure of it.

Even though she's in the third grade now, and he's still in nursery school, they continue to spend a lot of time together. They share a room, too.

The older kids roomed together as well, until my oldest son was about eight: then we separated them. It creates closeness to have children room together, and it saves time, too, because you can put them to bed at once. One isn't wondering if the action is all taking place in the other's room rather than theirs, which cuts down on jealousy. And if one wakes up scared in the middle of the night, the other is there for comfort.

▮ Save Your Positive Energy for the Right Employer

Now you have your beautiful baby, but you still need your job. What about that much-discussed juggling act—the baby/the office, the office/the baby?

First things first: it is best to work for a company that is at least kid-tolerant. One of my proudest legacies as an editor in chief was leaving behind a string of pregnant editors and new mothers at my magazines. Every woman who was a good employee before having children was just as good after coming back from maternity leave.

In fact when I was at *Marie Claire,* I had hired a talented young editor named Clare McHugh as executive editor when she was eight months pregnant. She worked right up to the baby's birth and returned a couple of months later, raring to get back into the swing of things. She'd been clear about her commitment to coming back to work after the baby was born, and I took her at her word, because of her overall enthusiasm for the position. Her timetable was stated up front, and she stuck to it.

When you become pregnant, it is important to be similarly straightforward about the situation to your employer. You can't be assigned to major responsibilities if your boss can't trust your commitment to your work. If you are ever in the position of interviewing for a job while you're pregnant, of course you have to be committed to your baby, but you also have to assure the employer of your commitment to the job. A lot of women don't present that commitment, because they are ambivalent. But your boss has a business to run, with deadlines and revenue expectations. Business is business. You have to understand that it's not just about you.

No one wants to replace a strong employee just because she is having a baby. Most reasonable bosses will be flexible to some degree, but it can't be give, give, give, or take, take, take, at either end. You do need a warm and empathetic supervisor, and that might be a man or a woman.

Think hard about how your boss and your company rate on the parenting scales before you enter the fray. Do women at the company have kids? Do they take maternity leave? Do they still get promoted when they return from the leave? Are they treated with respect? Do company higher-ups make pointed remarks about the women on leave? Are there raised eyebrows about a woman who is then pregnant with a second child? Do mothers make partner: is it that kind of firm? If you even suspect that the place where you're working does not look favorably upon having childbearing women on the staff, it may be best to look elsewhere.

Being Pregnant on the Job

OK, you did it: you have a job you love, you're at work, and you're pregnant.

How to cope?

Some days you may feel great, other days it's a struggle to keep your eyes open at your desk. I spent the first fourteen weeks of each of my four pregnancies sipping club soda all day long because I felt so sick.

For me, the first pregnancy was the most tiring. It may have been the shock of the new experience, or it may have been that once I was pregnant for the second time, I couldn't just come home from work and pass out on the couch. I had to play with my son, give him a bath, the works. I didn't have the option to collapse, so I didn't. It's amazing what you get done when you have to.

The last two pregnancies were particularly hard for me because around the fifth month each time, my back went out: I couldn't sit, and I couldn't stand. At one point when I was involved in the redesign of *Cosmopolitan* magazine, working with a small team away from the rest of the *Cosmo* staff, I was in such agony that I resorted to lying flat on the office floor until the spasms subsided. Did I look like a fool? Probably. Did my staff just step around me sympathetically and keep working? Thankfully, that's exactly what they did.

I just had to get the job done, no matter how I felt.

You do what you have to do, but bonding with other mothers who work can be an ideal way to get ready for life as a working mother. My friend Sharon conducts focus groups in different cities; I met her first on the train platform in our town when we were both commuting to our jobs while enormously pregnant. Our oldest daughters wound up being born two weeks apart, and both mothers and daughters are friends to this day.

I started hiring Sharon to do focus groups when I was at

YM, and later at the other magazines I edited. I remember watching her conduct a focus group from behind a one-way window. She was six months pregnant at the time, with her third child, and every night she would politely excuse herself at some point in the session and hightail it to the bathroom to throw up. Then she'd return calmly to pick up the discussion. She didn't let her physical condition interfere in her work in any way.

The only thing to do is to convince *yourself* that you're fine, and carry on. It doesn't help to focus on the nausea, your girth, your aches and pains. It's best to stick to your normal schedule. During my pregnancies, I was up and out of the house by seven, and at the gym by eight for a workout, five days a week. I couldn't work out quite as usual, but I did the best I could and was remarkably energized by it.

Be aware that when you start a family, there is no need to let your ambition diminish, as many women do. I think that's the wrong attitude, because when you get higher up the food chain, you tend to have more power about shaping your time off. The more senior and valuable you are to your company, the more power you have, and you are going to need the power and flexibility that come with that seniority.

■ Never Let Them See You Sweat

The key to being pregnant in the workplace and still winning points with colleagues and skeptical but sometimes silent higher-ups is to keep your cool at all times. You may be sick, tired, and hungry, but don't say a word about any of it to your bosses. Never complain. **Never let on that you are feeling less than perfect in any way.**

Employers do not want to hear about your nausea or your swollen ankles.

They don't want to know how tired you are, because they don't want to feel bad because they're making you work.

You are being paid a salary to work, and you are not in a life-threatening situation: pregnancy is part of the natural order of things.

Never call in sick unless you are really, *really* sick.

Don't talk much about the pregnancy in the office, period. If someone asks you how you are feeling, answer politely that you feel great, then change the subject.

If you've noticed, this is how Vice President Dick Cheney deals with questions about his heart problems. The only time he mentions them is when he is assuring the American public that *he is fine.* His message is that *he is invincible.*

So are pregnant you. **That lump on your belly has nothing to do with your job performance.** If you carry on as if nothing is different, you will impress your bosses that you are truly valuable, and worthy of support during not just the nine months of the pregnancy but, most importantly, the maternity leave afterward.

And if you really want to impress people in your workplace, don't stop working until it's time to give birth, pretty much literally. Better to be at work evincing power through pregnancy. I remember sitting in my editor in chief's office at *Flare* magazine in Canada on the day my oldest son, Noah, was due. I needed to call one of our major fashion advertisers about a special section I was working on. He was surprised to hear from me, and asked, "Aren't you supposed to be having a baby soon?"

"Yes," I told him, "my due date is today."

He almost dropped the phone. Not only did I get the information I needed; he also boosted his advertising commitment to the section. I felt great about getting his support for our special section and focused on that success rather than the discomfort I was in.

I went into labor later that afternoon.

I could never understand the impulse some women felt to take off two weeks or more before their due date. Who wants to sit at home waiting? You're huge, you're desperate for the whole thing to be over: sitting at home just makes the days endless.

At work you don't have time to focus on how huge you've become, or how many new double chins you now have. And don't give up your style just because you're pregnant: continue to wear high heels, and do not succumb to a "sensible" mom haircut that makes you look like you belong on the sidelines at a soccer game. You can go to those games when the time comes, and still look your best! Being pregnant should not define every aspect of who you are. It is just part of your very full and exciting life.

■ Make the Arrangements That Work for You

As a pregnant editor in chief of two major magazines, *Cosmopolitan* and *Glamour*, I didn't feel that I could just back-burner those magazines for two months on a maternity leave. I didn't feel that was fair to my company, fair to my readers, or fair to my staff. Also, in both cases, I'd only been there for a year or so, and I felt I couldn't leave after I'd had my baby. I needed to keep embracing both babies, not dump baby number one in order to take care of baby number two. So I negotiated with my company *not* to take a maternity leave.

I said, "Obviously, I can't work the day I have the baby. But as soon as I get home, I'll be back involved." And I was. I'm not embarrassed to say I was reading proofs in the delivery room, waiting. Not everyone may want to adopt this solution, but the point is to make your own choices in figuring out how to balance work with motherhood.

I was sitting there, and I needed to distract myself. So I kept working. Then by the time I got back home, I was ready to be back in touch. I worked from home for the first three weeks in both cases, and week number four, picked up and brought the baby into the office.

I certainly couldn't impose on the staff, so I brought a baby nurse to help me. I parked them in my office, and since I sat in the newsroom anyway most of the time, they were very much behind closed doors. I could run my company and be fully involved, and still nurse my baby. I could go behind closed doors when I was doing phone calls, when I was reading copy. I spent a good deal of time with my baby yet was still be able to be responsible for everything I needed to be responsible for.

Because I had agreed to take off only two or three weeks, rather than the usual two or three months, the company agreed to this arrangement.

Make your deal—whatever makes sense for you, whether it's taking a full maternity leave, working part-time from home, or working part-time in the office and bringing your baby in. But if you do elect to bring the baby in to work, understand that he or she can't become the center of the office.

When I was at Condé Nast, the company asked me to go on the road to meet some important advertisers when the baby was only a month old. I took the baby with me. The company paid for the baby nurse's travel expenses to accompany me. Companies are often willing to compromise and can rise to the occasion if you give them a chance.

Other companies will pay for women executives to take their baby and babysitter with them for travel, so they can attend important events, too. When I started out in the publishing business, there used to be a lot of events—conferences and advertiser events—where male publishing executives took their wives along. They'd go away to various islands for meetings, and it was very common for them to bring their spouses.

But now that there are so many women in the field, you

don't see them bringing their husbands. Nobody brings spouses anymore. So having a baby accompany his or her mother on a trip is perhaps less expensive than what these same companies used to have to put out for the nonworking spouse to attend.

The Double Standard and Other Unfortunate Realities

You read articles all the time about men who have wives and families; you never read critiques of them as parents. The issue is barely even mentioned, except when the men are so fabulous because they walk their child to school on the way to work or leave early occasionally to coach baseball. When male news reporters and anchors have to go on the road, no one asks if they'll bring their kids or feel guilty for leaving them behind.

David Beckham, the world's most gorgeous and famous soccer player, is celebrated because he walks his little boys to their nursery school. He got into hot water with his soccer coach because he went to parents' day at the nursery school, but the press celebrated him for putting his child ahead of soccer practice one day. His fans love that he made his child feel more important than anything else.

There is a double standard for women. Anything that's written about me mentions that I have four kids. The motherhood issue is always raised; it is speculated that maybe I'm not such a good mother because I have this career. How can I have time for my kids? When I was home before I went back to the office at *Cosmopolitan,* the *New York Times* sent a reporter to my house and did an article that really stuck the knife in.

The writer thought it was outrageous that I would have a phone headset so that I could talk on the phone to the office and hold the baby to breast-feed at the same time. Babies have been breast-fed under many circumstances in human history. I didn't feel guilty about it at all. I think the writer just needed a catchy "hook" for her story.

You have to focus on the fact that your baby is happy that you're there for him and you're happy that you're there for him.

Recently I ran into an old friend I hadn't seen in a while who has a very high-profile position. She was seven months pregnant. I said, "What are you going to do? Are you going to take any time off?" She guiltily whispered to me, "You know what? I'm really just going to take three weeks at home, and then I'm going to bring the baby to the office, like you did. Or I'm going to just do half days. I can't just disappear for two months because the place won't run right. But don't tell anybody, because you know, I don't want to have people talking about it."

Women who work always feel vulnerable about family matters because they are still competing in a man's world. And a child, whether it's your first or your fourth, can be seen as a major distraction from your job. That's why it's so vital to work for companies that have family-friendly policies.

Though some women may be afraid to ask for something "special" when it comes to maternity issues for fear that it makes them appear weak in some way, consider this: when you're out of the office for an extended period, your replacement may not be nearly as good, or as knowledgeable about the job, as you are.

I think most women would be surprised by how accommodating a boss may be. If you are valued by your employer—which you should be if you're doing a good job—most companies would rather have you back after a leave than have to hire a new employee.

When I was at *Glamour* and I was still breast-feeding my son Sasha, I would bring my breast pump to the office every day. One day I attended a luncheon in Washington, D.C., that the then-president's wife Hillary Clinton sponsored for female journalists and editors. Linda Wells, the editor in chief of *Allure,* also attended. She was still breast-feeding, too, which we realized when we ran into each other, both carrying our pumps onto the plane in New York!

The White House staff kindly made arrangements for us to have an office to visit a couple of times during the course of the day, where we could pump! So we excused ourselves from Hillary and went down the hall to our pumping station. It's a new world for working mothers, and even the White House knows the drill! Smart companies do, too.

5 Check Your Lettuce in the Coatroom: How to Manage Your Happily Unbalanced Life

▪ There Is No Such Thing as Balance

Please don't tell me about how much better mothers have it in France or Sweden. I don't live there and don't plan on moving anytime soon.

To people who ask me, "How do you do it all?" I answer simply, "I don't. **There is no such thing as balance.**"

Working mothers don't balance, they juggle, like performers in a circus. But circuses are fun, and so is the unbalanced life, if you approach it in the proper spirit.

So how do I keep up with the big job, spend time with my family, and nourish my marriage? I focus. Some would say that I obsess. Well, what's wrong with that?

Obsession Moves the World Forward

There is nothing wrong with being obsessive. What would have been accomplished in this world—medical breakthroughs, great inventions—without the power of obsession? The joys that both my work and family bring me fully justify the focus I place on each of them. There is nothing else I want to devote my time to. As far as I'm concerned, hobbies are overrated, as is that much-discussed condition known as "being well-rounded."

You Can't Be Great at Everything

Do what you're best at in an obsessive way, and everything else will fall into place. I was criticized by one of my former bosses for not being computer-savvy, but in the meantime I took his magazine from a $15 million loss to a $15 million gain, a swing of $30 million in a year and a half. So what's more important? Numbers talk. I have other skills that are more necessary to my work than computing. I can't be creative staring at a screen all day. It just doesn't work for me.

I also don't have a problem with talking shop when not

at work. I like to talk shop. A lot of people think you should leave the office behind when you leave work, but why? That's what you're interested in, so why not discuss it? There's nothing better than gabbing with close colleagues (most of whom become good friends) about your mutual obsession—your work!

■ The Unbalanced Life Does Require Sacrifices and Clear Priorities

There have been many articles and books, from *Perfect Madness* to *I Don't Know How She Does It,* that talk about women who had high-powered jobs and promising careers and gave them up to move to suburbia and focus solely on raising their children. Trying to juggle babies and briefcases became overwhelming for these women. It was exhausting; it was frustrating; they were guilt-ridden. They felt they couldn't do a good enough job as either a mother or an employee when they were trying to do both at once. So they quit work. But they were throwing out the baby with the bathwater.

The books and articles almost always applaud the choice to give up the career. However, for most women, this really isn't a viable choice, because only a very small group of women have husbands wealthy enough to support them and their children with one paycheck.

I'm not in that group. Luckily I love my work, but there are certainly days when I wish I could be the class parent, or be highly involved with the PTA, or take care of some of the things around the house that need doing. But the bottom line is that I can't, and I'm not ashamed. You shouldn't be either.

My wedding photos sat in a box in my closet for the first sixteen years of my marriage until a sympathetic photo editor heard about my situation and offered to put them in an album just because she was so appalled for my pictures.

Some things are really important, but so many things are not. My children are clean, properly dressed, and, thank God, studious and well behaved. So first things first: you have to prioritize, and you shouldn't have to make apologies for doing so.

Decide which people in your life really matter to you: your parents, your children, your boyfriend or husband, your best friend. These are the people who will truly miss you if you don't show up, so these are the ones for whom you should always show up for: your being home, or in their lives, means a lot to them.

Life is short; why worry, for instance, about social events you don't need to go to? Concentrate on what you absolutely must do, and forget about the rest of it. People spend so much time going to things because they think they must: then they find out that no one really noticed whether they came or not.

▪ Cancel That Guilt Trip!

What is the point of beating yourself up about not being the perfect mother or homemaker? I don't lie awake at night and kick myself for not helping my kids construct hand-beaded bracelets that day. If my son is happy as I push his stroller at the same time that I'm talking into my headset, then I'm OK with it, too. He doesn't seem to notice that Mommy's working, as long as I'm there to push him on the swing. If I felt angst or guilt being there with him, he would feel it, too.

Not everything can be of equal importance to you. Does your desk really have to be clutter-free at the end of every working day? Do you have to print out e-mails? Do the insides of your office drawers have to be pristine? You have to learn what corners you can cut, so that you can prioritize and spend your time at work and with your family wisely.

You have to make choices. If I want to have time with my kids, I may occasionally have to ruffle a few feathers in the office. I'm in a deadline-oriented business, and there are only so many hours in the day. Ten minutes spent on office gossip is ten minutes I don't have with my family. I don't consider myself rude, but I am rather straightforward. I have to cut to the chase and get what needs doing done. If I were a man, no one would expect otherwise.

Sometimes I just don't have time, for instance, to ask my staff how their weekend was. Sometimes people perceive me to be cold or uncaring because I don't indulge in chitchat. Of course if a staff member is ill or has gone through something serious like a divorce, I always make time to ask him or her how things are going—to be supportive. It's important to be there when the need is real.

◼ Ban "Perfection Guilt" from Your Brain

As you try to juggle in the face of every day's potential new disaster, it is important to remind yourself that you are not a bad mother just because you didn't make homemade Halloween costumes. Blame and guilt are useless responses to the issues working mothers face.

> **"What ifs" constitute a complete waste of time and energy. You can be passionate about both your work and motherhood, even if you are not perfect in either realm.**

A mother has to consciously take herself off her guilt trip and think more like men do. **Few guys beat themselves up about messiness in the household or about missing time with their family.** We have to take a few lessons from them and give ourselves permission to do what we want or absolutely need to do rather than what is expected. Men give themselves permission, for instance, to eat out of the can; to lie on the couch and channel surf; to go to a sports event with the guys; to do their jobs well but not perfectly. And they give themselves permission to enjoy their time with their kids—to play. They can leave the unmade beds and piled-up laundry behind and get out and enjoy themselves.

◼ Don't Parent by Guilt

I don't buy in to the idea that you can't be tough with the kids when they need you to be, just because you aren't spending more time with them. That's guilt working in a nonproductive way. Kids need to be disciplined when they act out, whether you've been with them all day or not.

You can't say to yourself, "Oh, I've been gone all day at the office, so I shouldn't give them a time-out." **Your responsibility, and priority, as a parent is to give your kids guidelines, whether you are working or not.** You can't let things go just because you don't see them as much as you would like to.

My husband and I make sure to schedule "alone time" with the kids. I take my younger son and daughter to karate class on Saturday mornings, for instance, and join the class myself. That way I am getting an additional workout, and spending time with my kids at the same time.

Or Michael and I will have the two older kids meet us in the city for dinner, while a babysitter stays with the two younger ones, Leilah and Sasha. Then we'll plan an activity for them at a later date. Maybe we'll go for a bike ride to the ice cream store, or we'll go to Central Park to ride the merry-go-round. The point is to make time for each of them to feel special.

Maybe you can't radically change your life, but you can look at it differently. **Making yourself feel guilty about being a bad mother, friend, or housekeeper does not make you better at any role.** So tune out your self-berating, depressing, critical inner voices. If you give the kids all the love, support, and encouragement you can muster, they will turn out to be good, happy kids.

■ Develop Flexibility

As a couple you have to develop enough flexibility to cope with different phases in your life and adjust to the family's needs accordingly. I'm usually up at 6:15 A.M. and out the door by 7 A.M., so my husband gives the kids breakfast. One of us arranges to be home by 7 P.M. most nights. We never take business trips at the same time.

You have to work with the situation you face. I've been known to leave my Manhattan office in the middle of the day and drive all the way home to Westchester for a teacher meeting or a key doctor's appointment. But I get back to the office in time to get that day's assignment completed.

> In order to have the full life, you have to have support. You can't do it all yourself. You need people in your corner whom you trust.

Most important is to do what your instincts tell you is best for you, your family, and your job—not what even your best friend says, or members of your family. I know that if my husband and I had allowed our extended families to interfere in our lives, as they often wanted to, we would have been miserable.

We aim always to emphasize the positive when we are together, even if things don't go as planned—which of course they rarely do. We've long ago learned to accept that if we plan a trip to the beach, it will rain when we arrive. I once got Michael a canoe paddle for Father's Day and invested in special paints so Noah and Sofia, who were about eight and five at the time, could decorate it for him. It seemed like a great idea until the kids started fighting over which color paint to use. They ended up in tears, refusing to make any pictures on the paddle. Michael and I had to laugh at the inanity of it. Kids will be kids. And as long as you learn to celebrate this fact—and not wring your hands over the lack of a "perfect" family life—you will be able to see what's important for you as a fulfilled woman, both in the home and in the workplace.

▇ Take Essential Short Cuts, and Check Your Lettuce in the Coatroom

Solutions for the overwhelming aspects of your life lie in being creative with your coping strategies, and not worrying about what other people think of them.

While it's true that the visibility of my job requires me to come to the office every day well groomed, with at least a modicum of style, there is behind the "glamour" a woman who shops for groceries on the way home from work at 8 P.M. and sometimes later. I've checked lettuce and other produce into the coatroom at some of New York's finest restaurants, where I'm having a business dinner.

And by stopping at the market on the way home, even if it's late on a deadline night, I accomplish two things at once: I feed my family, and at the same time at the checkout rack I keep tabs on the *Star* and other publications I oversee.

To make the best use of my time, I take some shortcuts that work for me. If I don't have time to make to-do lists, I leave phone messages for myself on the answering machine in the office when I'm away from it. Then when I come in, I can get started on the things that need priority attention. It's a useful memory jogger. I can't keep everything in my head, and I have so much paper to handle every day that sometimes a list gets lost in the shuffle.

There are other little things you can do as a working mom to help economize with time. For instance, when the kids get their photos taken at school, buy them. Buy extras for the relatives too; then you won't have to worry if you don't have time to get them taken professionally yourself.

I've even had pizza delivered to our town swimming pool for dinner, so that we can all have an outing, which feels like a special treat on a summer night. I call ahead from the train to arrange the delivery; then I meet the rest of the family at the pool. It's shortcuts like these that can turn everyday things into adventures and still allow you to do what you have to.

Don't forget that family and friends can get together with you and the kids at a local park. What's wrong with an improvised picnic? Turn obligatory family get-togethers into playdates. Kids hate to sit quietly in someone's living room. Get the whole crew out into the park, or to your local pool.

Mostly, though, the minute I get home, I attend to the children: playing with them, reading them stories, helping with homework projects, putting them to bed. Then my husband and I eat dinner, sometimes as late as 11 P.M., which turns out to be an ideal time to touch base and catch up with each other without the kids interrupting. Though our system may not work for every family, you *can* allow some leeway in making a plan and a schedule that works for you and your family. Though I may eat at odd hours, I am still doing my job, spending time with my husband, shopping for my family, playing with the kids.

Family meals are total mayhem. Getting everyone to sit down at the table together is a major accomplishment. When we try to have family dinners, it's hard to get everything plunked down on the table so that you can sit down for two seconds. With kids, someone always wants something else. The eight-year-old will not eat the same vegetables as the four-year-old. Then they all want chocolate milk, and I have to make it for them a certain way. And they all want to be heard, so they all talk over each other, in order to get attention. No one waits their turn to speak; it's a form of combat—who can get Mommy and Daddy's attention. My husband and I just laugh: there aren't too many Martha moments in our household.

We celebrate our noisy, full-throttled family meals instead of being filled with angst that they aren't *Parents* magazine perfect. We laugh at our eighteen-year-old son's newly blond hair; he wound up dying it back to its natural dark brown a few weeks later. So what if we don't get out of the house until 2 P.M. on a Sunday because we can't get it together until then?

There's nothing wrong with being a bit inventive, and a little unconventional. Who cares if your neighbors look at you oddly, or if your mother-in-law disapproves? You're tending to your family first, and keeping the proverbial balls in the air at the same time.

On weekends I concentrate on family: even a trip to the fruit market can be fun for the kids. Obviously my life bears no resemblance whatsoever to those of the women on shows like *Sex and the City*. I have no time for regular manicures, shoe-shopping expeditions, chatting on the phone with girlfriends, and catching up on the latest news. Sadly, my friends hear from me rarely.

The bring-it-on, over-the-top approach to life involves an extra level of energy and commitment; it isn't risk- or trouble-free. When you're keeping aloft the myriad details involved in a life that is one big juggling act, there are bound to be days when you drop the ball, when things go haywire. Sometimes it seems as if every day fits this bill. But there isn't anything you can't deal with.

Admitting that you can't be "perfect" and expert in all things, and that you can't accomplish everything on your own, is the first step in dealing with the tumult that sometimes threatens to engulf you. Don't let "unrealistic" expectations hold you back. And never forget that a sense of humor is the most essential tool of all, because if you can't learn to laugh off the things that shouldn't be at the top of your list of problems, you'll never enjoy what life really has to offer.

I'm always juggling so many things that things are bound to go wrong in every part of my life. On Saturdays, when I'm trying to get the kids out of the house, invariably after I get everybody in the car, I have to run back inside four times because I cannot remember to bring the juices and the water that everybody wants.

And I'm always forgetting things at the gym. I leave my house so early in the morning, when it's chilly, that by the time I've finished my workout, it's warmer. So I'll leave my coat at the gym. I'm forever calling: "Is my coat hanging there?" Yes. "Did I leave my watch in my locker?" Yes.

It is not the end of the world to be a bit discombobulated. I manage to get to the gym, as well as to be with the kids, and to participate in my community. So what if things go a bit askew along the way?

This roll-with-the-punches point of view is particularly important when you're on the road with the kids.

During a recent ski vacation, for instance, I was jolted awake by a call from one of my senior staffers, distraught over a small item that had appeared that day on "Page Six," the gossip page of the newspaper the *New York Post,* claiming that members of my staff had been having "secret meetings" to complain about long hours and other issues at the magazine. Though I knew this wasn't true, and that the brouhaha about it would pass quickly, my day of so-called relaxation had begun on a somewhat unnerving note.

After fielding more calls from the office, I finally got the kids ready to go up the mountain for their ski classes, and my husband and I were off to our lessons, too. Barely a third of the way down the first run, the cell phone chirped yet again: it was the clinic at the ski resort, reporting that my then-seventeen-year-old son Noah had just broken his wrist snowboarding. As I raced down to find him and gather up his medications, there was yet another call to inform me that my younger daughter, Leilah, was throwing up at the kids' center, Camp Snowbird. She had contracted stomach flu.

This was not exactly what we'd had in mind when planning our mountain "escape from it all" vacation.

■ Let Your Kids Play in the Dirt

At many points in the lives of our kids, they didn't care if they were in the Middle East or the heart of London. All they wanted to do was play in dirt. They spent hours in a magnificent playground in London that commemorated Princess Diana. We saw London *without* the museums. On a trip to Israel a couple of years before, they spent all their time in the playgrounds there, despite the best efforts of our tour guide.

Sometimes all you're going to see are the parks of the country you're in, and you have to be content with that. On a trip to Washington, D.C., all the younger kids wanted to do was play in the gravel—literally—on the Mall. That was it for them! And of course hotels are excellent for the pool, the room service, and for ordering up movies.

Instead of following a rigid itinerary, I simply chose to enjoy our chance to be together as a family. You can stress a lot less as a parent if you too can learn to enjoy sitting in the gravel.

My husband and I try to take the same perspective about the kids in general. We don't push them too much in any particular direction. They have to motivate themselves. Luckily, they all have a strong work ethic at school: they go above and beyond.

◼ A Routine Can Anchor You and Free Up Time Better Spent Elsewhere

Given the number of balls you'll be juggling on the way home or to the office, it helps to maintain a routine. OK, so you know you're not Miss Perfect. Sticking to a routine helps ward off some of the usual elements of loserdom and disaster. For instance, if you go to the same place each morning for your bagel or your workout, or schedule certain key meetings for the same time each week, you'll feel more secure because there are fewer opportunities for things to get messed up.

If you follow a routine, you don't have to spend energy reinventing the wheel every day after you get up. But the demands of your routine shouldn't take up too much of your day, or you'll get locked in.

A routine can enforce a good habit. For example, if you are up at 6:30 every day, giving yourself time to go to the gym, it becomes such a habit that you can't imagine not doing it. It becomes wired into your day, and if you skip it, you're way off-kilter. It's a positive form of addiction, in a way.

I hate it when I'm scheduled all day with back-to-back meetings, because then if something goes off schedule, I have no breathing room to deal with problems. A strong routine gives you some space between key meetings or appointments and helps you manage it all, especially when you factor kids into the equation.

There are many things about my working life that I have to leave routine-free. As an editorial director of celebrity newsweekly magazines, I'm at the mercy of the news and of the drama of the business I'm in. Not to mention the fact that this friend or that parent has a crisis, small or large—an argument with her boyfriend, a messy divorce, two competing job offers, or a cancer diagnosis. Things happen every day that demand your attention and you have to adjust. Having a lot that is normal and routine stabilizes you to deal with the things you can't control.

You Are Not Your Purse

Despite my basic routine, I have no clue how some women hew incredibly tightly to their schedules, are up at the crack of dawn, and manage to arrive at 8 A.M. breakfast meetings looking blown dry and perfectly manicured.

I am more likely to sleep through the alarm, then scramble to get my bag together, with the rings, bracelet, and watch getting thrown into the wallet—no time to put them on now. I had a ring designed to hold all four birthstones of my children. It's my prize possession.

First race to the gym, and since there's never enough time to get perfectly put together before my first meeting, accessory and makeup application will have to happen in the taxi on the way to work. Aside from my purse, the carryall into which my work files and gym clothes are deposited is hardly an Hermès: it looks more like a gym bag, and is stuffed to the gills with copy and magazines and clippings for story ideas, to the point where the whole thing provides a major workout for my shoulder before I even hit the office.

Legendary *Vogue* editor in chief Anna Wintour supposedly once said that a woman should carry only a small clutch bag because a shoulder strap ruins the line of the clothes. Mine isn't just ruined, it's obliterated. I'd call my on-the-way-to-work look more Ellis Island than Fifth Avenue.

The substance of what you do, and who you are, is what defines you, not whether you sport the season's chicest clutch bag. I have more important ways to spend my time in the morning than agonizing over my choice of tote.

That isn't to say that looking good is not important: it is. But it's not the only thing. And you don't need one of those $1,500 pocketbooks that celebrities carry, or a pair of Manolos, to look your best. There are plenty of pretty, inexpensive knockoffs. It's all about the flair with which you present yourself.

There are women out there who never split a seam or speak in anything but a charming manner. I've seen them; I've even met them. They just aren't like me, or maybe you. The rest of us spill coffee, usually in the immediate vicinity of a white blouse freshly unpacked from its dry cleaning wrapper. Even if we can't change our ways, we can learn to protect ourselves and prepare for all contingencies.

Assuming that sartorial disaster is always around the corner, for instance, I always have backup, such as a pair of extra shoes in the office, in case the heels to the ones I have suddenly break off, as mine have! If you anticipate more of life's day-to-day disasters, and prepare accordingly, you'll sleep better at night.

I'll never forget the day I was to lunch at the Four Seasons restaurant, New York City's premier "power lunch" venue, with my colleagues at *Us Weekly*—the publisher and the beauty director—and the president of Ralph Lauren's fragrance company. I was in the middle of a frantic morning, lunch was in fifteen minutes, and there was no way I could be late. Nor was there any way I could show up the way I was, with my makeup long worn off and my all-black outfit littered with pieces of mysterious, highly visible white shmutz.

Throwing some supplies in a small white paper bag, I raced to meet my colleagues at the elevator. Once we hit the inside of the town car we'd reserved for the occasion, I opened my coat, stretched out my toes, reached into my bag for the lint brush, and started to roll it up and down my outfit.

Us Weekly publisher Vicci Rose was horrified: "What are you doing?"

I explained my plan: while they went to the table and made the proper introductions, I would hightail it to the ladies' room to brush my hair and apply the requisite makeup. Within a few minutes I was at the table, smiling and presentable; only my coworkers and I knew what a frantic struggle it had been to get me there. If my life were less hectic, I would have spent more time on my appearance, maybe, but would the results have been better? I doubt it.

To keep those all-important outward appearances up, I find it helpful to keep a stash of things in my desk at the office, not just a pair of backup shoes. For instance, I have

an extra pair of pantyhose
extra makeup
a nice purse to take out at lunch, given that the bags that I schlep in every morning are not terribly presentable
lint remover
a can of anti-static-cling spray
feminine hygiene supplies
a brush

In addition I keep extra forks and knives and salt and pepper for impromptu meals. I even keep a ski jacket in the closet in the office because the air conditioning can get so intense in the summer. Because I have to go to evening events, I have a blow-dryer on hand in the office, as well as a nice black top in case I spill something on myself during the course of the day. My office is in effect my home away from home.

If you can't carry these with you at all times, at least have them in a desk drawer in the office.

Simple black V-neck T-shirt or sweater To replace white or any other light-colored item of clothing that has magnetically attracted coffee, lipstick, salad dressing, or baby spit-up.

Thong You thought you checked for VPL—visible panty line—in the mirror before you left for work, but who can see at 7 A.M. anyway?

Toothbrush and dental floss To take with you for meals out of the office. Check for spinach in the teeth *before* leaving restaurant.

Tape and safety pins For hems that come apart inconveniently midday.

Extra pair of black sling-backs Or any other shoes you can wear with almost anything in your wardrobe, to replace favorite shoes whose heels slide off mid-step and send you flying across the room.

Razor and blades For quick underarm repairs—in case you forget on those mornings when you're wearing a sleeveless garment.

Small hand mirror Carry in purse at all times to

deal with lipstick on teeth and windblown debris on face.

Breath mints

Surplus tampons and pads Be prepared, and don't wear white when you know the day is approaching! Have one of each of these in your purse and gym bag at all times.

Hand towel Why is it that when you try to remove spills with paper towels from the office bathroom, you wind up with the spill, plus bits of the paper towel all over your outfit? Use a hand towel instead.

Comfortable flats or a pair of athletic shoes and socks For traipsing long distances around town in case of transit strikes, citywide blackouts, or rush-hour traffic.

Umbrella Of course it always rains when it's not supposed to, so you need to have one of these on hand. But be prepared to replace it, because you know you'll leave it in the back of a cab or a bus or at an appointment before you know it. If you can, buy these in bulk.

Flashlight and batteries Who knew that a tree branch could cut off the power in half a country plus part of Canada? Next time you'll be prepared.

Band-Aids and Advil

There have been times when I felt like I was holding my life together with safety pins, literally and figuratively. What's wrong with that? A wise person once said to me, "Inside, you may be a frazzled woman whose hem is held up with a safety pin or tape, but remember that the only person who knows this—or cares about it—is you. Your secret is safe as long as you don't go on a megaphone and yell, 'I'm a mess!'"

And once you pull it together on the outside, you'll feel pulled together on the inside, too.

Don't Forget the Romance

Last but certainly not least, there's the issue we all face on the home front—keeping the romance alive between you and your boyfriend or husband, even in the midst of the madness that especially family life entails. How do you stay in love?

First of all, you've got to marry the person who wants to be with you, who is as madly in love with you as you are with him or her, and who doesn't have you cast in a certain role, like that of the trophy, or his substitute mom, or the piece of arm candy. This is the person whom you can have this full life with, the guy who feels like he got a great deal the day he married you! And you've got to feel the same way about him.

If you're looking for a guy with a big bank account—if this is why you choose this guy, and he chooses you because you're a good "social" or "looks" match—then just accept that you're not going to have a wonderful, crazy-in-love marriage. You may have a marriage that still works, but it will be more like a business partnership. It's not a choice I could make, but there are other women who can, and that's fine for them.

So how do you keep romance alive? It helps to marry someone with whom you share goals, ethical beliefs, and hobbies. For example, my husband and I love to spend time together because we enjoy so many of the same things. Despite parenting four children and keeping up demanding work schedules, we don't merely live parallel lives. We love to hang out together. We look forward to skiing, camping, and canoeing; we garden, hike, bike, and cook together. It's easy for us to have fun. And that keeps the relationship stimulating and also gives us lots of time to talk. We have tremendous respect and appreciation for each other.

After twenty-two years, my husband and I really are still in love. Of course we get angry with each other. Sometimes we fight. I think it's OK to argue as long as you're not doing it *all* the time. You've got to let it out. If you're upset, it's bad to hold it all in.

But on the other hand, we don't hold grudges, and we do forgive pretty quickly. There are couples who walk around for two weeks without talking. We never would have had four kids and lasted twenty-two years as a married couple if we acted like that. I don't think either of us has ever had a serious moment where we thought we would split up.

My husband and I rarely have time for so-called getaway weekends—maybe once every five years. This is where my personal guilt comes in. I don't feel guilty about going to work all day, but I don't like to leave the kids on the weekends. I don't want vacations without the kids. I remember when my parents would go away on vacations without us; we hated being left behind.

I think my husband feels the same way, even though he's home more. He doesn't like to leave the kids either. Hardly a full night goes by without a child in our bed, or maybe two or three. We're so used to it at this point that we don't even know what life would be like if we went for a week without them!

We used to work late and then go out for dinner, just the two of us. I guess you'd call it a date night. Now since I'm working with weeklies, constant deadlines make it very hard. I just want to be home when I can. I'd rather have a romantic dinner at home after we put the kids to bed, even if it's at 10:30 or 11 at night.

Another reason our household functions amid all the chaos of life with four kids is that my husband and I don't have what I would call control issues, where one person is trying to control the other. I think that's huge. With a lot of couples, there are control issues that include weird money matters. We only have joint bank accounts. What I earn is his; what he earns is mine. And in my case, I've been the breadwinner for a lot of years, and I don't give it one moment's thought.

He takes care of the household bills. Whatever money he needs, he takes. I never even look at it. And I think that you've got to be like that. If you're going to fight and divide up money, and bicker over who spent what that week, the atmosphere can get poisonous. If you're on a budget, then you're both on a budget—as we've been many times. We're still on a budget.

Of course you have to marry someone you can trust financially, who is not going to go and empty out your whole bank account. It all comes down to trust. **If you lack the trust, you'll try to control.** Where's the joy in living this way?

The full life, though sometimes overflowing with joyful madness and mayhem, is the only one worth living.

6 You Can't Be Great for Everyone: Sticking to Your Mission

a t this stage in my life, I know that I can't make everybody happy. If the readers of my magazines are happy, if my boss is pleased with my performance, if my family is healthy and well cared for, then everything else is secondary.

Girls are still raised to be "nice." When you get into the work world, you still want to be liked. **The truth is that it's more important to be a good person than to be a good girl—to be someone who will do what she thinks is the**

right thing, even if it doesn't result in instant popularity with peers. You can't please all of the people all of the time, nor should you aim to.

I get people riled up. For example, as soon as I got to *Flare* magazine in Canada and began to redesign and reconceive the publication, a negative backlash ensued. It was my first experience with eye-rolling employees. Many people fear change and won't make the changes necessary to adapt to new management or new goals. When you're changing a product, sometimes you have to change the staff producing that product. I was forced to let a lot of people go, which is never a pleasant task. But you've got your mission, and you have to stick to it.

I'll go places others don't want to go—or don't dare. I don't say to myself, "I'm going to get everybody worked up." I'm not one who loves to stir things up by nature, but because I'm usually hired to "fix" a situation and improve results, inevitably I am shaking up the status quo.

If you're doing what you think is the right thing in your job, you can't worry about the whispers that may follow you when you change the way things have *always* been done. Gather your allies. Stay strong. Find employees who will help you achieve the desired results. Remember that you may not win popularity contests if your goal is to do what the boss wants done. He or she is the only one you need to please.

As long as your boss is happy, as long as you've got his or her approval or sign-off, then it's safe to go ahead. You have to be willing to take responsibility for your actions, even if they create a big to-do. If you're absolutely convinced that you're acting in the best interests of the company, and the boss is backing you up, then do it!

Taking the Rap

I clearly remember playing a game outside as a little girl in suburban Toronto. I must have been seven or eight years old. I was with a pack of neighborhood kids, and we were knocking on people's doors and running away and hiding. We'd ring the bell, then dash away. Usually, no one was home. However, at one house an older woman threw the door open right away. All the other kids ran, but I didn't move. I just stood there frozen, meeting her eye to eye. For some reason, I felt that I just couldn't run; I had to take the rap for what we'd been doing.

The woman eyeballed me and yelled, "*What* are you doing?"

I said I was sorry. She yelled at me for a couple of minutes about how I was doing a bad thing, and that kids shouldn't behave like that—and how dare I disrupt her day, and so forth. I just stood my ground, and apologized again, and heard her out. I couldn't cut and run. I felt a responsibility to face the consequences of our actions.

Taking the rap is what you've got to be prepared to do if you want to move up the food chain and into the realm of taking responsibility. When the buck stops at your desk, you've got to make decisions in the best interests of the company or business that are not always going to be popular with everyone.

When you make changes, you're going to have a lot of critics. Some people are constrained by the thought of that; for better or worse, I've never been held back by those worries. If I am hired to do a job, as far as I'm concerned I'm given the go-ahead to take on a mission, and I've been willing to take the heat in order to get the job done. Set goals for yourself, even if you can't achieve all of them overnight.

If you want to get something accomplished, you may put other people's noses out of joint. It's important to be in a field that you love, because there will be some rough days. Everyone who's worked with really top-notch movie directors says they can be difficult, for instance. But when you're sitting there in the audience enjoying a great film, do you care? Nor does the relationship between the cast and the director have any effect on box office receipts. Sometimes I've had to ask people to work long hours. When you change a magazine or start a new one, you work really, really hard. At a weekly newsmagazine, you're going to work longer hours than at a monthly. But I've never been more demanding of my staff than I am of myself. I'm working the hours right alongside them. If they're toiling away, I'm toiling away.

I would never want to be abusive. I've never been a screamer, nor do I ever want to humiliate people. But I will ask staff to produce the best work they've ever done. And if people work hard, they end up succeeding. If they do a good job, they're going to get promoted; they're going to make more money and in turn create more opportunities for themselves.

■ Do What You Believe In Long Enough, and You Will Get Results

I like my readers. They are the people I need to please, and I don't care who they are. I am thrilled to have them, whether they live in a trailer park or on Park Avenue. I am deeply grateful to anyone who reads one of my magazines. I am over the moon to be chosen by my readers, and I want to hear from them and know what interests them. They are the people I answer to.

When I went to *Glamour,* everybody assumed I produced a sexier magazine there, because the newsstand sales went up, and people assumed that's all I knew how to do, having come from *Cosmo,* where my mission was to revamp the vamp. My staff did increase the sexual content of the magazine, but only by a tiny amount. We did more stories about relationships with men and about sexual issues, because the readers wanted more on those topics. When I got there, I felt that *Glamour* had an anti-man attitude. Guys were the enemy; they were out to hurt and abuse and use you. I felt on the other hand that most women wanted a good relationship with a man—a loving, positive relationship. So *Glamour* became more man-friendly; some viewed this change as my being a traitor to the sisterhood, but I was trying to create a bigger and more popular niche for the magazine in the marketplace.

At the same time, my staff and I tried to have fabulous women's issue stories. We were the first to talk about the plight of women living under the Taliban in Afghanistan in 1999. *Glamour* was—and still is—the only women's magazine to have an editorial page, and my first editorial was about how women in Afghanistan were being treated terribly under Taliban rule. In the piece I encouraged American women to fight for the rights of these women, who couldn't even go to school. We partnered with the organization the Feminist Majority to raise awareness of the issue in the American press, working with Mavis Leno, Jay Leno's wife, who spearheaded efforts to get the American government to pressure the regime in Afghanistan to improve the lives of its country's women.

Additionally, we sent reporters to Kosovo to interview young women—the same age as our American readers—who were living in refugee camps during the war with the Serbs. Educated, articulate in several languages, these women were often professionals. I wanted our readers to understand that "there, but for the grace of God, go I." We also did features on female genital mutilation in Africa. I was very proud when as a result of these features *Glamour* won an Amnesty International Award for magazine journalism on women's issues.

At *Glamour* we also investigated how women were

treated at home—for instance, what harsh treatment they received, under the drug laws in particular, because they didn't necessarily have information to trade for a plea bargain and lighter sentences. We actually helped to get four or five young women out of jail. We wrote about one woman who was in jail for a crime she didn't commit, and we initiated a letter-writing campaign on her behalf. In another instance, we learned about a forty-year-old woman in California who had already served twelve years of a mandatory, no-parole, twenty-four-year sentence for helping her drug-dealer ex-husband get his bail money.

She'd wired him money in Germany—where he'd been living after they split up, and where he was arrested—from a bank account he'd told her about. After she did this, federal agents pounced upon her as an accessory to the crime. Naïvely, she didn't even know that her ex-husband had become a partner in a drug-producing and -selling operation overseas. At the time, the state where she lived, California, had very tough drug-related laws on the books, similar to the Rockefeller laws in New York State. The judge even apologized to this woman, then twenty-eight, as he sentenced her to twenty-four years in jail for her mistake.

Glamour readers became her advocate and started a Web site for her cause. After President Bill Clinton pardoned her, she came to our office, and we took a picture of her with all of the people on the staff. She thanked us and explained that she had always desperately wanted to have children. She was still young enough to conceive; if she'd served another twelve years, she would have been too old to do so when she got out of jail. I could barely choke back my tears as I gave her a hug.

I also wrote to President Clinton about five other young women who were also implicated in their boyfriends' drug crimes and as a result received very harsh sentences. President Clinton pardoned all five of them right before he left office. That was about as gratifying as it gets!

On the one hand, I was getting vilified in the New York press for supposedly making *Glamour* sexy; on the other hand, the people who were really reading the magazine and saw the kind of stories that we were doing felt that we deserved the Amnesty International award. I concentrated on what I thought were the best interests of my readers and ignored the naysayers who could only talk about the "sexy" cover lines.

■ Even If You Don't Get Immediate Results, Keep On Trying

At *Us Weekly* I took the heat, this time for doing a new kind of celebrity journalism. The magazine had been more traditional and entertainment-oriented before I arrived, more like *Entertainment Weekly.* Its other chief competitor, *People,* featured celebrity styles and antics in just a small photo section in the front of the magazine and had other small celebrity features, but most of it was about real people. I had always enjoyed European and British magazines that focused exclusively on the lives of the stars and had lots of fun photographs throughout. I just knew there would be a market for a publication like that in the U.S.

I fashioned *Us Weekly* into a weekly celebrity news-magazine that had some entertainment but really focused on the lives and the looks of the stars. I emphasized their fashion style, their beauty looks, their homes, and what they looked like when they weren't in front of a TV or movie camera. That's what I wanted to read, and so did my customers. Intuitively, I knew my readers wanted to see celebrities as they looked and behaved in their everyday lives.

On television, there were already shows like *Lifestyles of the Rich and Famous* and *Access Hollywood*. The equivalent just didn't exist in the magazine world. I was interested in the lifestyles, lovestyles, and lookstyles of the rich and famous in Hollywood. When I say "Hollywood," I mean it not as a place but as a world. Though readers loved what we were doing at *Us Weekly,* and circulation continued to rise, I once again faced criticism for lowering journalistic standards, because I wasn't producing a magazine with the traditional format of one lengthy article after another.

Now celebrity news is so ingrained in the culture that no one can remember when we didn't hold our collective breath to find out if Brad and Angelina would end up getting married. When Tom Cruise gets engaged, it's the lead story not just in *Star* and *People* but also on the *Today* show and CNN. On newsstands, celebrity interest is a phenomenon that has exploded in the past four years: one out of every five dollars spent on magazines now goes toward the purchase of a celebrity newsweekly.

I've been criticized for creating publications that are as addictive as candy: reading them is like eating a giant box of bonbons every week. I've been criticized for running shorter articles, for writing "charticles," and for placing every little bit of celebrity life under the microscope. *Star* has been called "a different kind of porn."

Well, if it's just so delicious that people really love to read it, I am not unhappy about that. I think it's a compliment that it's addictive. I am going to give the reader what he or she really wants to read, and what I want to read, and what's fun, entertaining, and/or helpful.

And *Star*, which I oversaw, can only break a big celebrity news story such as Brad and Jen's marital crisis, Britney's pregnancy, Ben Affleck and Jennifer Garner's engagement, or Angelina and Brad's romance, by using multiple sources and serious reporting. We have a high bar to get over before we can print a story. We have to make sure it's true.

Recently when a television interviewer asked me if I was responsible for the death of serious journalism, I just laughed. "Well, as a matter of fact," I said, "I don't see that there's any death of serious journalism. Both the *New Yorker* and *Atlantic Monthly* had record-breaking newsstand sales in 2004. They're doing very, very well."

And Editor in Chief Joe Dolce and his whole team at *Star* take what we do seriously. Maybe celebrities aren't serious as a subject, but we approach them seriously. We make sure that our reporting is excellent and accurate, and that it's fact-checked. We have to build our credibility. With every issue, *Star* becomes more and more credible, and it has earned a reputation for breaking celebrity news before any of its competitors.

The High, the Low, and Everything in Between

Why can't you choose what you want to read? Why should you feel bad or inferior because what you want to read entertains or amuses you and informs you about a not-so-serious subject? I don't think there's any crime in that. In fact, I think it's healthy. People need to blow off steam. They need to have fun in their lives. They need to escape for a few minutes. Women escape into *Star* the way men escape into the sports pages. And they feel the same need to keep up with the stars' antics that men do to read the latest scores.

And just the fact that a woman—or man—reads *Star* doesn't mean that he or she isn't also reading literature. We all have multiple parts of our personalities, as well as multiple aspects to our lives. It's fun to mix the high and the low, the cheap with the expensive. It's like wearing a Gap T-shirt with a Gucci skirt.

Because of cable television and the pervasive influence of the Internet, not to mention magazines and newspapers, we all know a lot about celebrities, so we can all gossip about them. It gives us something in common to talk about: whether you live in Florida or Utah, you know about Brad Pitt. In order to get out into the public arena these days, you almost have to be a celebrity, whether you're George W. Bush or Britney Spears or a celebrity doctor who makes a major breakthrough. It's all about the big personalities, about finding out who they *really are* versus just what they've done in their careers.

The covers that have gotten everybody talking about the new *Star* are the stories about celebrities' huge makeovers. Our readers love them. I think these stories humanize celebrities and make our readers feel so much better because they can see that celebrities aren't perfect. Not even they have a professional hair person and full-blown body makeup every day. Phew!

Ultimately, I really believe that *Star* and the other celebrity newsweeklies do more to build celebrities' careers than anything else. We give them fabulous publicity. We make our readers interested in them and their lives. Movie stars have always had to deal with public interest in their lives. They have since the 1920s, the era of silent films. If they didn't have it, they wouldn't be movie stars.

At *Star* we don't usually commission photos of celebrities—only occasionally. And there are certainly things we won't buy, such as "stalkarazzi," pictures that are taken from a great distance of stars sunning topless on a boat or photos looking into celebrities' homes. We don't take pictures of the children of celebrities without their parents, or of the children's schools. We don't buy photos of celebrities taken in a reckless manner. There are boundaries, and we observe them.

■ There Is No Such Thing as Perfect

In the magazine business, reader feedback is essential. When I was at *YM* we had discussion groups with teenage girls. Every couple of weeks, we would have a class come in, or just a group of girls, and we talked to them about what they liked or didn't like. In one discussion about models, the girls said, "We're sick of reading about models who are so perfect, and have perfect skin and perfect legs and perfect this-and-that. We want to read about models who wake up with big zits on their noses. We want to hear about models who fall when they're on the runway."

My staff and I figured out that these girls loved it when the models were publicly embarrassed: it made the readers less unhappy with their own imperfections. So we came up with a column where readers could tell stories about their own embarrassing moments. Donald Robertson, *YM*'s creative director, and I had gone to see the movie *Say Anything,* one of the best teen movies of all time. So we decided to use its name for the column. By the end of the week that the first column appeared, we had thousands of letters from readers, sending in their embarrassing moments to share.

We had really touched a nerve. "Say Anything" became

the most popular column in the magazine. Nobody had ever seen anything like it before. It made the readers feel better about awful things like having a Tampax string hang down from your bathing suit, or sneezing and having snot come out of your nose in front of everybody. We took a chance on a new feature readers seemed to love, and it paid off. Our newsstand sales and subscriptions went up and up and up.

We were proved right. Our idea proved itself in the marketplace, and when it did, our competitors started to copy the column. Now almost every teen magazine has one like it.

The *Marie Claire* reader was motivated by fashion, but it was a different kind of fashion than the sort then on the market. We came up with endless ways to show both high-priced *and* budget looks. Up to that point, fashion magazines hadn't featured low-priced alternatives to expensive designer looks. And we invented features like "Splurge versus Save"; "Essential Pieces to Have for Under $100"; "All the Essential Pieces for Your Fall Wardrobe for Under $100"; and "How to Wear an Outfit 7 Different Ways."

It was all about presenting fashion in very practical terms, because that's what *that* reader was fixating on—how fashion would work for her. It may not sound like the reinvention of the wheel, but at the time it was really something innovative.

Showing how to get a high-fashion look for less hadn't really been done then in any major way at any of the major fashion magazines. This was in the early 1990s, before *In Style* and shopping magazines like *Lucky*. The fashion magazines of the time—*Vogue, Harper's Bazaar,* and *Elle*—were doing traditional fashion shoots, scenarios, set either in the studio with models or out on location. They didn't shoot a lot of close-up photos of clothing, accessories, and beauty products. At *Glamour,* my team expanded the "Dos and Don'ts" throughout the magazine. When I got there, "Fashion Dos and Don'ts" were limited to the back page of *Glamour.* I found out a day after arriving at the magazine that this feature, shot in black and white, had actually been faked: the staff didn't really go out on the street and shoot real people. They set up a lot of the shots using staff members. So we changed that and did it all with real people, in color, at least a full spread in every issue. We'd also do big sections of dos and don'ts applied to your love life, and so on. We expanded the dos and don'ts concept throughout the magazine. Then every few issues we'd do a giant, multi-page section of fashion or beauty dos and don'ts, often with themes like "denim," "coats," and "hair."

The other thing that really worked for *Glamour* is that it was the only magazine at that time that was paying attention to "figure fixing"—dressing just for *your* figure type: how to get the right jeans for *your* body type, how to get the right skirt and the right proportions overall. These features responded to the readers' figure anxieties and gave them suggestions about how to look their best. Circulation numbers increased dramatically.

When I was at *Us Weekly,* I loved looking at photos of celebrities in their daily lives—getting a parking ticket, picking up their dry cleaning, taking out their garbage, carrying a tray full of coffee from Starbucks, pushing their kids on the swing. I thought it was fascinating to see celebrities being just like us. So I came up with this regular spread every week called "Stars Are Just Like Us," and it clicked.

I also came up with the Buzzometer, which measured what was buzzy—what was new and being talked about. I introduced little bees as a rating; if something really had buzz, it could go up to five bees in terms of how hot it was. Other popular features included "World News of the Week," which was like a takeoff on a newsmagazine, and "Celebrity Look-alikes," featuring celebrities looking, for instance, like dogs or politicians.

Because sometimes we didn't have enough access at the start at *Us Weekly* to the real inside story, we improvised. If a celebrity couple were getting married, we'd morph his and her face to make kids' faces on the computer, so we could see what the children would look like.

I was right in suspecting that people wanted to have a laugh and be entertained. We focused on young celebrities, unlike *People,* which had an older, more traditional look.

Today there are an ever-growing number of players in our category of celebrity newsweekly. *Us Weekly* sells close to a million copies per week. *Star* sells about 900,000 copies a week on newsstands, plus we have 600,000 subscriptions. *People,* which has been around for over thirty years, still leads with around 1.4 million sold on newsstands. There's an enormous jockeying right now for stories and for newsstand sales. Celebrity-based news is just part of our pop culture now, of our landscape.

At *Star* we went from a tabloid format to a glossy magazine. Younger women, the next generation of readers *Star* needed, couldn't be convinced to read it as a tabloid. They only began picking it up in droves when it became a glossy magazine in April 2004.

Taking the magazine from a tabloid to a glossy format was the hardest thing I've ever had to do in my career. People had preconceived ideas about what *Star* was, but the terrific editorial team has changed that. The facts were that the *Star* had been declining in sales to readers for twelve years on the newsstand; it carried very little mainstream advertising; the mean age of the reader was over fifty; and when I'd go to focus groups, people would tell me they thought it was about little green aliens. For all these reasons, *Star* needed to be reborn.

Now we've already launched a spin-off for *Star,* a new weekly lifestyle magazine called *Celebrity Living,* focusing on homes, fashion, beauty, shopping, entertaining, diet and exercise, wellness, travel—all the totally glamorous areas of celebrity life.

◾ Stick to Your Mission!

Wherever I've gone, the publications have done better than they were doing before I got there. And when I've left them, they've been in much stronger shape. Sometimes the improvement has been dramatic; other times it's been more incremental. But there's always been a steady increase.

Though you may have to step on toes to accomplish your goals, you also need to praise those who are doing a good job. It's important in the working world to be polite and considerate and to manage down as well as up. **You have to treat the men and women in the mail room with as much respect as your bosses and your boss's assistant.** People at all levels of the company can contribute to your success.

The trick is to be respectful and at the same time to be proactive, to take the initiative and not let other people—especially your critics—define your agenda for you and steer you from what you know is the right path for you. And you have to be willing to share the spotlight and the kudos with the people who work for you. Let the ones who are making your job easier know how much you appreciate what they are doing. Never take people for granted.

To be an effective manager in any kind of business, you can't sit back and just wait to be noticed. You have to stick your neck out and take the steps that will put you where you want to be. You can't stand on ceremony in today's world. It's too competitive out there.

As an employee, if you have an idea or a suggestion, be

bold, and take a chance. The worst that can happen is that the boss won't give you the go-ahead. But believe me, most bosses are impressed with any employee willing to go the extra mile.

■ Use Negative Feedback as a Motivator

Projecting confidence in yourself and your ideas is key because once you've begun to achieve some success in life, you'll come up against smack-down artists, people who are threatened by your enthusiasm and ambition and positive energy. You'll have to learn how to ignore them.

Don't let the smack-down artists derail you. You already know about the nasty inner voices in your head; the smack-down artists are the naysayers and the doom-meisters in the outside world, ever ready with a warning or a negative aside. They can be your coworkers, your colleagues, or critics in your industry. They may criticize you behind your back, or they may go public with their comments. In either case, remember that it's all too easy to be hard on yourself. Don't let others join in the fun.

Usually naysayers run out of steam at a certain point or get bored and find other worthy targets.

You are not obligated to listen to negative or disheartening comments from people; they aren't medicine, as in "good for you." Constantly absorbing negative things about yourself will definitely make you feel bad. Why wouldn't it? If someone is always telling you that you can't possibly be good enough to do this or that, or that your unique way of doing things is wrongheaded or silly because it is different, eventually you will lose your motivation and confidence.

If you let yourself get preoccupied with the negative voices from within or without, you will be holding yourself back from achieving your goals. Sometimes you have to literally stop talking to people who get you down, even if they're close colleagues or family members or friends. You can always put down the receiver on the phone or not make that date for lunch.

Just don't forget the sometimes heartbreaking truth that smack-down artists are not necessarily people in a far-off city but the people closest to you, the ones who really know where to stick the pins: the colleagues you've outgrown; the boyfriends or husbands who want you to be the support staff in *their* lives, not the leading lady in your own. They can be parents or siblings, or anyone whose own dreams may have been thwarted and who resents seeing you do well.

As you gain confidence in yourself, both in your career and your personal life, you will attract greater numbers of smack-down artists, because the better you do, the more you threaten people who are less able and who think and operate on a smaller scale.

If you let these people win—no matter who they are, or how much they profess to love you—you will never be happy. You'll be frustrated and depressed. There's a real difference between genuinely useful criticism and negative, soul-destroying attacks. You'll know the difference instinctively. Try to keep your focus positive, even when it isn't easy.

Be All Ears for Constructive Criticism

The exception to the criticism rule is listening to the people you respect and for whom you work—in other words, your boss, your clients, and the people who buy your products. In this case, you are indeed obligated to pay attention to what is said. Sometimes a boss will dish out soul-destroying criticism that is intended to make him or her feel empowered and to make you feel like a squished insect. If this is a regular occurrence in your work life, you probably need to start looking around for a new environment that offers more opportunity and is less soul destroying.

However, not all criticism is negative, and your boss may actually have your best interests in mind. When he or she is delivering constructive criticism, it's important to pay attention. **You can't get ahead if you can't overcome your defensiveness enough to listen to constructive criticism.** This is an important point: you need to be absolutely open to it. And the operative word here is *constructive*. You and your boss have the same goal, so why not listen?

I would call criticism constructive if it comes from a positive place to begin with. Almost always, someone who wants to give you this type of feedback starts with a positive: "You're doing this aspect of your job so well. Let's focus today on what we can improve." Or "I can see that you're really trying, and here are a few ways in which you might do even better." Or "I appreciate your efforts, but . . ." A person giving criticism this way wants you to absorb it in a positive way; he is making his intention to be helpful very clear.

So you should listen carefully, and follow up on the suggestions made in a specific way. Every boss has his or her own ways of doing things, and you have to honor this fact.

Don't react with excuses and in a defensive manner when you hear criticism. Instead, digest it. The boss does not want to hear all your reasons why you did something in a way that didn't work for him or her: he or she *really* wants to hear that you've genuinely heard what was said and plan to act on it promptly.

If the criticism is particularly hard to hear, breathe deeply, and resist any temptation to be rude or overly emotional. If you can't help the tears from welling up, excuse yourself so that you can pull yourself together. Acknowledge to the boss that he or she is not the reason that you're crying. Say something like "Sometimes I have a hard time controlling my tears, but I'm taking this conversation seriously. Let me take a few minutes and then come back and finish our talk."

■ Some Decisions Come with Costs

Leaving *Cosmopolitan* magazine was the hardest decision I've ever made. I simply knew I wasn't going to be the right editor for *Cosmo* for the next ten years. Despite the fact that I had succeeded there, I couldn't see myself remaining inspired over the long term in the way I needed to be in order to challenge myself to keep going to the next level. I felt I had a better chance of doing that if I moved to *Glamour*, which I felt was a better fit for me.

Even if you've been successful in a job, don't get complacent. Keep your mission in sight. Sometimes you have to risk a move to a place where your long-term growth prospects are better.

In today's world, it's sometimes hard to figure out where the middle ground is for yourself as an employee. How can you show loyalty and get a reputation as a solid, reliable person without being stepped on? If your needs or desires don't mesh with those of the bosses at your company, you are not necessarily going to be treated with kid gloves when you leave.

■ When You Leave, Leave Right

When you do leave, do so on the best terms possible.

■ Give as much thought to getting out as you did to getting in the door.

- Leave your work in good order, and give proper notice—a minimum of two weeks.
- Pass along your projects and explain them.
- Ask your boss what he or she wants you to get done before you leave, and do it. Don't agree to get things done before you go and then not do them. Live up to what you say you're going to do.
- Remember that life is long. Don't give an exit interview where you trash your boss or the company.
- Don't bad-mouth the company in general either. Professional exes are *not* the same as romantic exes, even if they, too, have broken your heart.
- Even if you're angry, keep your anger to yourself. Consider your work life a trash-free zone.

Learn this from one of my mistakes: if you have a contract or a very clear commitment with a company, don't try to back out before the end of your committed tenure, unless there are extenuating circumstances, such as illness. I had no such excuse; I was being treated well and was working with a great team. I shouldn't have caused my then-current employer any grief. I paid a price, as you'll see in the next chapter. I alienated people in a major corporation I can't go back to now—never a good strategy.

◾ Admit a Mistake If You've Made One

Don't be afraid to admit that—Omigod!—you've made a huge mistake. You've left a great job on good terms and taken the leap to a new place that is just not working out. Maybe the job isn't a good fit with your skills; maybe the position isn't what it was described to be in the interview; maybe the new company culture just doesn't feel as though it will be *your* culture. In any case, you're missing your old job and your old company—*bad*! If you want to go back, *do it*! Suck it up and call your old boss. If you did great work there, and the position is still open, there's a very good chance that your ex-boss will be thrilled to take you back. *Star*'s photo director Darren Walsh did just that when he worked with me at *Us Weekly*. He had performed fantastically there in the number two spot in the photo department. Then he was lured away to a photography agency. He'd been gone all of three weeks, and we were missing him terribly, when I got a phone call from a very quiet Darren at the other end of the line.

"Is there any way I could have my old job back?" he asked quietly. He was miserable in his new situation.

I was only too happy to welcome him back. It wasn't the first time one of my employees had left, only to make a call shortly thereafter wanting to come "home." Sometimes even if your old job is no longer available, employers will make room for you in the organization because they value you so much. If you've left on good terms, doors remain open to you.

Though it's important to stick to your mission in order to succeed, it's also important to be honest with yourself and admit when a correction is needed or a mistake has been made. People who know what they have to offer in the workplace will be strong enough to admit when they've made an error, and correct it.

Similarly, it is essential to admit when you're wrong and to apologize to the person you've offended, inadvertently or otherwise. When you're in a pressured situation, it's easy to be a bit short or to step over the line somehow, in terms of professional etiquette. **It is almost as important to know when you're wrong as it is to know when you're right.** We are all wrong at times. Be mindful of this fact.

Don't waste time getting your back up or rationalizing your behavior. Apologize, and move on. Failure to apologize can drive wedges between you and your colleagues. An effective boss or employee sees the bigger picture and knows that it is always better strategy to cooperate with coworkers than to alienate people.

In a similar vein, if someone in your workplace is offensive to you in some way, call it to his or her attention, politely but firmly, or the problem will continue. Sometimes the coworker isn't even aware of what he or she is doing.

And it is never too late to apologize or to thank someone for a favor done, or recognition given, or a piece of mentoring advice that really helped, even if you didn't realize its importance at the time it was given. An apology, like a word or note of thanks, is always appreciated, even years after the fact. And if you can master the art of making friends out of former enemies or adversaries, you've really come full circle.

At each step of the full, committed life, a proper ending to that stage, whether it's personal or in the workplace, is clean and honest and not shrouded in bad feeling. Then you can set out on a renewed path, rather than finding yourself in a dead-end situation.

7 Eating Humble Pie, Even at the Ritz: How to Come Back from Personal and Professional Disaster

■ Failure Is Only a Temporary Condition

I've made mistakes. If I could have read some of the advice I've given you in the last chapter, rather than living through the events that taught me what I know now, perhaps I never would have been fired from *Glamour*. At the time it happened, I thought I was finished. But as it turned out, this was far from the truth. What I learned is that **failure is only a temporary condition.**

As singer Mariah Carey put it recently in the *New York Daily News,* "Nobody can have a long career without experiencing the downside—some failure. But you *have* to remain positive. Because if you don't, your sadness will lead to bitterness and will fester into something ugly and unproductive. I think ahead. I never look back." After being declared "over" in the wake of several unsuccessful projects, she ended up riding the top of the charts with her most recent album *The Emancipation of Mimi.*

Rare individuals can actually rise above it all and thank an employer with whom he or she parts ways, for the opportunities provided, despite the fact that the situation did not work out. Though you may not have been right for that particular job, you may be right for something else that develops down the line, or for freelance work, or a special project. Why burn bridges if you can avoid it?

Trying to take this approach, I met with my then-boss at *Glamour,* Si Newhouse, the chairman of Condé Nast Publications, who was gracious when I was let go. I had genuinely enjoyed working for him, and I admired his tremendous enthusiasm for his magazines. I hoped he would remember that I thanked him for the opportunity he'd given me.

I'd been working in New York for the past decade—a period of economic stability—and like many people in my generation, I had never been let go. I can now say that once you've been through it, it's like you're in a club with the other people who've experienced the same thing. The club grows bigger every day, given the structural changes in the media and other major businesses.

When I was fired, I was completely shocked and unprepared. I'd been focused on working hard at *Glamour* and coping with the demands not only of my job but also of my two-month-old baby boy, Sasha. I had no backup plan. It was a very lonely experience as well. After all, you come to the office every day; you don't recognize how much of your identity is tied up in what you do professionally, when you've had a career that is your passion. And you also don't always recognize how social it is, until you don't have it anymore. The whole routine you've built for yourself goes out the window. You've seen to it that your husband and children have full lives, so you can't expect them to fill in the blanks for you. They give emotional support, of course, but that's all they can do.

When I told my family about the firing, my daughter Sofia, who was then about nine, was disappointed that she could no longer come to the office and hang out with the beauty editor and get makeup from the office stash. Still, she said quickly, "Don't worry, Mom, you'll get another job, a better job." The next morning she told me not to read the coverage of my contract nonrenewal in the *New York Times*, which carried two columns about my fall from grace and speculated on every conceivable mistake I might have made, a report all delivered with what seemed to me at the time to be glee. I had lost not just my job but also my "touch." I had "gone cold," several news articles speculated.

Friends advised me to take on a press person of my own to counter the bad coverage, but it was too late. I thought I'd never work again as an editor in chief, given the press coverage of my firing. No one reported that just four and a half months before I'd been let go, *Glamour* finished up the year with the biggest newsstand and advertising sales and overall revenue in its history. Oh, well.

I hadn't seen the writing on the wall, and now I was paying the price. I felt as though I had the word "naïve" branded on my forehead.

Being fired from *Glamour* was a devastating experience. I was so tied up in my job that not having my contract renewed was a huge blow, especially in such a high-profile position. Looking back, I see that I may have been disloyal. When I was one year into the job, I was approached by my previous employer, Hearst Publications, which owns *Cosmopolitan* and *Marie Claire* magazines, about returning to the company to head up *Harper's Bazaar,* their fashion magazine.

I shouldn't even have entertained the idea for a second. It was the wrong thing to do, because I was contracted to work for *Glamour.* But I allowed myself to be swept up in the excitement of a dream job. I had long been fascinated by *Harper's Bazaar,* and I felt there was a great opportunity to recharge it.

I was also open to the idea because I felt that at *Glamour* there was a lot of resistance to me. The editor who preceded me, the legendary Ruth Whitney, had held the editor in chief job for thirty years. She was revered. The moment I was announced as her successor, she told the *New York Post* that she thought I was a terrible choice for the appointment because I had been editor in chief of *Cosmopolitan,* historically *Glamour*'s rival publication and a magazine that was considered sexier.

Coming from *Cosmo,* I was regarded with skepticism by many staffers and some advertisers. It was a hard year for me at the magazine, and by the time Hearst made their approach, I was wondering whether Condé Nast might be happy to see me go.

After I got an offer from Hearst, I told my boss, and he was horrified. He didn't want me to go. I heard him loud and clear: that was the end of that. I had a contract. Almost two years went by, and not another word was spoken about it. Then I was let go, and I'm sure that the offer made two years earlier played into it. Talking to Hearst and entertaining the offer made me look disloyal. It was a terrible mistake.

To this day, no one in the magazine industry—except the top executives at Hearst, of course—believes that I did not keep talking to Hearst Publications after that initial overture. But I didn't. I didn't even speak to old friends at Hearst about anything to do with work, for fear of starting rumors.

When I realized I had behaved inappropriately, I quickly made amends, recommitting fully to *Glamour* and apologizing to everyone concerned. But the damage had been done, and I had lost the trust of my boss. We all make mistakes, but perhaps yours can be less dramatic than mine, if you remember that blatant disloyalty is never the smart course of action.

In the two years between the *Harper's* episode and my demise at *Glamour,* I did not keep up my antennae the way I should have. I missed important signs that the guillotine was about to come down. I had noticed certain odd things but dismissed them as silly or incidental. They weren't. Why, I wondered, at an awards ceremony had I been exiled to a table where there were no other of the company's major magazine editors in chief? I also noticed that the company did not seem very empathetic regarding my stint of nonmaternity leave, when I brought my fourth child, my son Sasha, to the office rather than taking a real leave. I had failed to make my boss happy; failed to provide for my family; and failed to protect my own career and my position. Boy, had I messed up!

You have to remember that with a little bit of distance, most mountains will be revealed to be mere molehills.

At *Glamour* I also had some internecine problems within the company. We had done a really nice cover shoot with actress Catherine Zeta-Jones when she was still an up-and-comer; this was before her marriage to Michael Douglas and her starring movie roles. She was very happy with the story, and she really liked the cover. We got great feedback from her team.

A year later she had a big movie coming out, and she'd just tied the knot with Michael Douglas, so she was very much in the news. We'd shot a new cover for the magazine—not featuring her—that just wasn't great. I had the idea to look through some of the old film that we hadn't used from the other shoots during the course of the year, to see what we had on file. We came across our wonderful photos of Catherine Zeta-Jones in different outfits from our previous cover shoot. She looked the same as she did a year later. Given her new high profile, we figured that we could do a really nice story on her and her new movie, and use these pictures, which we had a legal right to do. When I contacted her PR person to ask if Catherine would do a new interview, her rep said no.

We decided to go ahead with the cover anyway. I discussed it with my immediate boss James Truman, then editorial director of Condé Nast, and he was fine about it. When it came out, however, there was a big controversy, because Catherine Zeta-Jones was not happy. She and her publicist had not controlled what we were doing.

As it turned out, she had a cover coming up two months later on *Vogue* magazine. In the meantime, our cover sold through the roof. I took a drumming in the media press, from "unnamed sources," about running this unauthorized cover. I read in the press that *Vogue*'s editor in chief, Anna Wintour, was upset that we ran this cover before she ran her cover. To me all this feels like ancient history now: three years later, the concept of only running a cover of a celebrity who fully cooperates is truly quaint. Neither *Star* nor *Us Weekly* nor any of the other celebrity newsweeklies makes it a practice.

■ When Something Bad Happens, Don't Get Beat and Bitter, Get Busy Fighting Your Way Back

I couldn't have been job hunting at a worse time, because the economy was starting to go into a major downturn, which for magazines translated into the most devastating loss of ad pages and revenue since the Great Depression. My phone didn't ring, and weeks turned into months.

After I lost my job at *Glamour,* I had to make some calls that required me to conquer my inner good girl, the one who doesn't like being pushy. It isn't easy to call people you have never met and ask them for a meeting. The inner voices telling me that this wasn't ladylike behavior were in full force for me at that time in my life, vulnerable as I was in the wake of being fired. I decided that it was absolutely necessary to take a proactive approach, so I spent hours networking with friends and acquaintances to assess how my skills might be applied to other businesses, since I was doubtful that my career in magazines could continue. For me it was best to cope with being unemployed by creating a routine to follow, so I took the train into the city every day and went to an office provided by Condé Nast in an outplacement company.

If you wind up unemployed, I would recommend that you negotiate with your former employer for outplacement services if you are in a position to do so. I was lucky enough to have an office with a computer and a phone and a fax, and there were friendly people willing to help me redo my resume and give me advice. I hadn't written a resume in years. **I worked all day, every day, at finding a new job.**

For months I wondered if I would ever get hired again. It felt hopeless. Every road I went down appeared to dead-end. No opportunity that looked real materialized. Then came the disaster of 9/11, and the economy went into a free fall. No one was hiring. I had loved working in the magazine business, but I was virtually convinced at that point that those doors were now closed to me forever. I would have to re-create myself.

I pitched myself as a magazine consultant and landed a three-month gig with Meredith Publishing putting together the prototype for a lifestyle magazine I'd been thinking about for years. It ended up being called *Living Room*. I sold the idea of this book to publisher Simon & Schuster. I wrote an article about the future of fashion advertising for a publication that covers the fashion and ad businesses. I developed the concept of a new cosmetics company with my former beauty editor at *Glamour*, Veronica Hinman. We also came up with an idea for a new kind of spa and with several ideas for TV shows. The job offer that seemed the closest to coming to fruition at that point was in a related business, the fashion industry.

When we're happily employed, we all fantasize about what we'd do if we had more free time or other career options. Now I had the time—though not in the way I would have chosen, or imagined. I tried to make the best of it by thinking creatively, "outside the box."

Job hunting had supremely difficult moments. I'll never forget my interview with the CEO of one magazine company I'd previously worked for very successfully. I was trying to sell myself as an editorial director. This CEO told me that I had no value to him: I felt smacked on each cheek. My experience was worth next to nothing, he said. One person is just as good as the next, and everyone is replaceable, he seemed to be saying to me.

Maybe we all feel like cogs in corporate machines some days, but even cogs are not all identical. Interestingly, this man was gone himself in a fairly short time. It turned out he had a lot of his own problems.

I continued information-gathering meetings with people: those who helped me were like lifeboats for me. It was a journey; each person I met led me to the next one. And if I hadn't set up those meetings, where would I have been? Moping around the house? Only you can find yourself a new situation, even if you have others to assist you and cheer you on.

When someone finds a new job after looking for a

while, people say that he or she has "landed." They're on solid ground after swimming or floating in the great blue sea. **Most people I know who got fired wound up in a better place, or on a new path. So did I.**

I persisted, and in the end I did find a job where I could make a real difference. And as it turned out, it was in magazines. After almost eight months of being unemployed, I heard that legendary magazine editor Jann Wenner was looking for a new editor for *Us Weekly*, a formerly monthly entertainment magazine that he had re-created as a weekly, which was still striving to find its identity. When I first tried to move back to New York City from Canada, I had actually interviewed with Jann Wenner at what was then *Us* magazine, a monthly. At the time, he didn't think I had the experience to do the job, and he was right.

My first interview with him on a Friday went well, and I decided to show how eager I was, so I spent the weekend creating mock layouts for *Us Weekly* magazine—ripping, tearing, and pasting bits of type and photos to demonstrate my ideas. I sent my dear husband to Kinko's at 2 A.M. to make color Xeroxes of the mock-ups, which we dropped off at Jann's house on a Sunday, so that when he went into the office Monday he'd have a clear notion that I could meet deadlines as well as generate ideas for his publication. At our lunch the next Tuesday, he offered me the job.

Sometimes your lowest point can push you to your highest point. The *US Weekly* opportunity came along unexpectedly; it was like nothing I had ever done. And under my leadership, the magazine took off. In a little over a year, newsstand sales more than doubled—from 274,000 to 600,000 a week. I ended up being named Editor of the Year by *Advertising Age,* a prestigious honor in my industry. (I was the first person to receive the award twice, because I had also been named Editor of the Year when I was at *Cosmo.*)

Jann Wenner threw a fabulous party at the Four Seasons here in New York for me; he was very generous. He invited the other editors in chief and publishers of all the other big magazines and newspapers. I remember looking around and thinking, just a year earlier, I had been let go from my previous position. In twelve months I'd gone from the lowest point to the pinnacle.

People warned me about going to *Us Weekly,* which was struggling in its transition from a monthly magazine to a weekly. Some naysayers worried that I wouldn't have enough of a chance to turn it around—that it might be closed down if I didn't succeed instantly. Well, first of all, I was unemployed, so I was willing to take that risk. For several years I had had an idea for a celebrity-filled newsmagazine just like this. Now I had a chance to execute it. So here was a positive result of being fired: I was able to move on a creative idea I never would have been able to take a chance on if I had stayed in my stable job at *Glamour.*

Though we were understaffed the first several months, and the *Us Weekly* team was also less experienced at news gathering than our chief competitor, *People,* we succeeded by being creative with limited resources.

For instance, when Julia Roberts got married to cameraman Danny Moder, her official wedding photo went not to us but to *People.* So we took a still photo from her film *The Runaway Bride,* in which she wore a wedding dress, and put it on our cover. We tried fun, offbeat approaches to the story, asking an astrologer if the union would work out, and having a photo illustrator create baby pictures of the couple's potential offspring. We even sent a team to Taos, New Mexico, the site of the wedding, to take photos of plastic lanterns and chairs that we found out were used in the "down-home" ceremony.

We made *Us Weekly* an alternative in attitude and outlook—younger, hipper, and more fun, with a good sense of humor. We were more daring, more irreverent, more fashion-oriented, and just plain funnier than *People.* My boss Jann Wenner was supportive of everything I and the *Us Weekly* editorial team wanted to do. I was thrilled to have come on board.

You can be kicked to the curb and still climb back up. Failure is not a permanent condition. Failure is only *temporary.* If you persist in reaching back up, you will get there sooner or later.

It's best to adopt a realistic attitude. In order to start climbing, you may have to accept some setbacks along the way. After I was fired, I wasn't expecting to be rehired at the salary I'd been making at *Glamour;* I needed to get back to work. I took a job that entailed a large salary cut, but I got incentive bonuses based on sales. Though I had fewer perks at *Us Weekly,* a lower budget, and a smaller staff, I made it work. I saw the job as an exciting opportunity. I needed someone to give me a chance at that point, and Jann Wenner did.

A little over a year later, I received a second key opportunity from David Pecker, the CEO of American Media. My contract renewal discussions were bogged down at Wenner, and David Pecker had his own important mission—revitalizing *Star.* The highly successful tabloid had lately been struggling with the competition from the new glossy celebrity weeklies—*Us Weekly* and *In Touch,* another entrant into the quickly growing field, which sold for the bargain price of $1.99.

His company, American Media, owned other tabloids, such as the *National Enquirer* and the *Globe,* as well as a number of highly respected health and fitness titles—*Shape, Men's Fitness, Natural Health,* and *Muscle and Fitness.* I was offered the job of editorial director for the entire company, with my first major priority to reinvigorate *Star.* It was a tremendous opportunity to grow professionally, and I leapt into the process, which led to our transforming *Star* into a glossy, mainstream magazine with a growing circulation and healthy advertising base.

When a Crisis Hits, Keep Moving, Despite It All

A crisis is a character-defining moment, whether it concerns a job or the death of a loved one or illness in the family. One thing I've learned from being fired and from my problem pregnancies, and my mother's bout with kidney cancer, not to mention the trauma of having one child who had a brain tumor and another with leukemia, is that you can be in a situation so terrible that you think that it is all over—this is the worst you can imagine—and then you find out it isn't. You can get through these things. You can survive them, and so can your children and other family members. You can get help. Modern life and medicine are full of miracles. And people, including you, are full of resilience.

When my daughter Sofia, now fourteen, developed a brain tumor at age three, it was a life-threatening crisis; she had to be rushed into emergency brain surgery. Fortunately within a week of the discovery of the tumor, we found out that it was benign and that she would survive. It was terrifying, but with the work of an amazing pediatric neurosurgeon, Dr. Stephanie Rifkinson, Sofia made it through two twelve-hour brain surgeries.

It was even harder when Leilah, our younger daughter, was diagnosed with leukemia at the age of five, because her struggle went on so much longer, and there was less of a defined sense of when it would be OK. Though she is now in remission, has been chemotherapy-free for over a year, and all her blood tests have been normal, I still worry about her every single day. When your child has a serious illness, you learn about a different kind of coping.

I found out about her cancer while alone on a business trip in Chicago at 10 P.M. one night. My husband called with an oncologist on the line. I was stunned and physically shaking as I received the news that our daughter, who we thought had a virus, was in fact most likely suffering from a leukemia or lymphoma. Immediately after hanging up, and in tears, I called a close friend who fortunately turned out to have a brother who was a specialist in blood malignancies. He gave me a great deal of information.

I learned quickly that in a crisis, you have to educate yourself as to the nature of the problem. You have to ask a million questions.

At six the next morning, I flew back to New York after a sleepless night. Michael and I went directly to Columbia Presbyterian Hospital with Leilah for a consultation. Our pediatrician had set us up with a wonderful treatment program led by Dr. Michael Weiner, head of pediatric oncology at the hospital. He started Leilah in treatment for acute lymphoblastic leukemia—the most common form of childhood leukemia—that day.

It's horrible to see your five-year old so sick. She'd first become ill while we were on vacation, skiing at Snowbird,

Utah. She was pale and tired—just not herself. When I took her to the Snowbird clinic, the doctor thought she had a virus. Mother's instinct told me that things just weren't right. So I went back to the clinic a few days later. This time the doctor was concerned that she might be getting pneumonia, so he did a chest X-ray, which showed a large shadow around the area of her heart. He advised me that this wasn't normal for a five-year-old, and he wondered if she had an enlarged heart a congenital defect, or an infection.

I could tell that this doctor was trying not to freak me out, but it wasn't working. I speed-dialed my pediatrician, who returned my call pronto even though it was a Sunday. He told me not to worry; it was probably just an enlarged lymph node caused by a virus, he explained. Nonetheless we flew right home and then raced the next day to the doctor's office, where he was so reassuring that I didn't cancel my overnight business trip to Chicago. The next morning my husband took Leilah for an MRI and blood tests, just to be safe.

What the MRI ended up showing was that the circle on the X-ray wasn't an enlarged heart, but a mass of leukemia cells in her chest wall. She also had masses on her hips, which are typical of leukemia, a blood cancer.

■ Act Quickly and Decisively

Once Leilah was settled in at the hospital, Michael and I launched into action. We gathered more information, explored other treatment options, and compared notes with other specialists. We did our research until we were comfortable that we were getting her the best treatment possible. It helped us to cope, that we knew we had her in the best hands. I think I would have lost my mind if I hadn't had tremendous encouragement not only from my husband and family and friends but also from Dr. Weiner, who told us the first time he examined Leilah, "I can cure your daughter." I clung to those words.

Because her illness was discovered very early after the doctor at the ski clinic did that first X-ray, my daughter had a much better shot at a full recovery from a very fast-moving disease. My gut had told me that Leilah wasn't right, and I had listened to my inner voices and taken action right away.

Michael and I were rigorous in following doctor's orders. She never missed a pill; we did everything the doctor advised. During the first year of her treatment, every time her fever spiked above 101, we had to take her to the hospital. She'd stay there until she recovered. That meant that either my husband or I was there with her at the hospital 24/7. Even with radiation, the chemo, and other drugs, she didn't miss too much school. We wanted to keep life as normal as possible for her.

My daughter needed treatment for a full two years; that's the protocol for her disease. Now she's been out of treatment for over a year and is checked every three months.

We were privileged to have the support of friends, family, and neighbors during this time. They brought us meals and took care of the other kids. They pitched in to give my husband a break from the stays in the hospital; he'd quit work to take care of Leilah, and I was supporting the family. I had been at *Us Weekly* for just three weeks before Leilah was diagnosed: I got the job in the nick of time. I don't think I could have coped with looking for work while my daughter was so sick.

Many people in the press didn't have much sympathy for me in this situation. In fact they seemed to think it was crass or unseemly of me to keep working long, hard hours at such a time. But we were going through a family crisis, and I couldn't worry too much about what reporters had to say. I needed to reboot my career after my exit from *Glamour*, and I still needed to support my family since Michael couldn't possibly work, not to mention the all-important fact that I needed to maintain our health insurance. Anyone who's ever been in a new job, still unproven, when a medical emergency in the family hits knows the importance of good health coverage.

If I'd been a man, the fact that I worked in a high-profile position and was striving for the success of my magazines would not have been news at all. And no one would have written a mean word that I had a very sick child at home.

My husband and I did what we had to do to cope, day to day. I had to shut out the whisperers and meet my professional commitments, as well as deal with our family's problems. During the first few intense months of Leilah's treatment, I just kept doing my job and running up to the hospital as often as I could. Sometimes we didn't close the magazine until after midnight, so I'd race to the hospital on my lunch or dinner hour. Or I'd go very late at night, on my way home.

It seemed that we practically lived in the hospital; we were there to be Leilah's advocate, to read to her or keep her spirits up, or just to hold her hand. On weekends I'd take the Saturday night shift and stay over there, snuggling with her in her hospital bed.

It was then that I learned that you shouldn't be stoic if you're really in a bind. You can't be afraid to let people know the nature of your predicament. In turn, you have to give back and help people if they need you, too. Even little things can make a difference.

At the same time, you can't cave if people are depending on you. You've got to keep thinking, and moving. You can't roll up into a fetal position and stay in bed. If you have a big problem, such as a very sick child, you can't worry too much about little details or annoyances: the crisis puts things in perspective. I am now just so grateful that both my daughters are healthy that every other problem pales in comparison. I don't have much patience for people who whine about small things.

You can be in the darkest place and still have hope. When you are first punched in the stomach with horrific news—like the fact that your child is going to require serious brain surgery or immediate treatment for leukemia—you are devastated. When my daughter Leilah was dangerously ill, I called the doctor regularly for assurances that she was going to be OK. His words kept me sane. If you keep the sense of hope inside you, you can go on, and even move forward. You can even learn from these experiences and grow as an individual as a result, just as they say in the old saws about one door opening when another one closes. It's true.

When both of my daughters were ill, and when I got fired, I found it enormously helpful to keep up my workout routine as much as possible. Not only does exercise help you keep your spirits up, but you have that routine to fall back on, to remind you what your normal life feels like. New studies have shown that an hour of cardiovascular exercise three times a week is just as effective as drugs in combating depression.

At each of these times, I felt like I was swimming in a vast ocean with no horizon line in sight; I thought I would never find a job ever again, that our family would always have to worry about Leilah. But in each case, I acted quickly to inform myself, and I stayed in the game. I learned that if you do, something will come your way.

■ The Good Side of Repression

Literally refusing to think about whatever it is that is getting you down can help you feel better. If it sounds like I'm saying that you should learn to compartmentalize, to repress negative thoughts and emotions, you're right. I absolutely believe that there is value in not wallowing in depressing or terrifying thoughts.

In fact the worse the situation you face, the more you have to section off your brain so that you can deal with what's ahead of you, day by day. You have to balance the crisis with the practical facts of your life. This is especially relevant for long-term crises. I had to go to work every day for the two years that Leilah was sick. If I'd allowed myself to dwell to excess on the seriousness of her illness, I would have collapsed completely. Instead each day I got up and did my job. That was my coping strategy.

Immersing yourself in your work at a time of crisis, whether it's about a sick child or a broken heart or the death of a loved one, can bring enormous relief. Fixating never helps. Focusing on danger and negative possibilities can literally make you sick.

Shrinks have a word for this: *catastrophizing*, which means taking every scary thought that comes into your head and following it to the nth degree. By doing this, you make the danger even bigger in your mind than it is already in reality. You make yourself more fearful, more paralyzed, and less able to act.

That's why **I have come to believe that repression is good!** It is the opposite of catastrophizing. Even now, I have to repress my scary thoughts during Leilah's continued recovery, because there's just no other way to get through them.

Don't Inner-Fixate

I know that many of our pop psych icons preach that you should delve inward for the answers to your problems. If you're upset, confused, or depressed, the answer is to retreat into some meditative experience and think about your issues. In other words, take a huge amount of "me time." Sometimes there is wisdom buried in your subconscious that may just need "quiet time" to emerge. However, I believe that too much of this "inner spacing" can be bad for your mental state.

You don't necessarily already have "the answers"—whatever they may be—in the core of your being, waiting like treasures to be excavated. Why would you? Chances are that what you need is advice from someone with more experience, training, or expertise to help you. And just thinking, and thinking, and then thinking some more can become counterproductive and narcissistic, not enlightening.

In order to get through hard times, don't inner-fixate. You have to keep reaching out and looking for lifeboats. Talk to people who've had the same experience and have gotten to the other side of it, have survived it—whether it's being fired, going through a divorce, having a sick child, or being sick yourself. Support groups can help too. And always get as much information as you can about the situation you confront.

> Lifeboats won't float to you. You have to inflate them yourself or swim out to them. Don't be afraid to show vulnerability. It is only when you do that that others will help.

■ When in Doubt, Throw Out a Life Preserver

Don't forget to lend a hand to others. Even the smallest gesture can mean a great deal to someone who's going through a crisis. When Leilah was sick, people surprised me in the way they reached out to me and to my family. I was touched by all the expressions of support we received. One colleague sent dinner to us at the hospital every night for a week, for instance.

After I was fired from *Glamour,* a book agent friend sent me a copy of the book *When One Door Closes, Another Opens.* It was a life-changing work.

When you hear about a friend or colleague in trouble, don't hesitate: take action, because he or she may be reluctant to ask for help. If a friend has broken up with a boyfriend or lost a spouse, take him or her out for Valentine's Day. Kidnap a troubled friend on a Saturday night and go to the movies or out to dinner. Do something thoughtful that shows you are thinking of him or her and the situation. Try to help fill this new void in your friend's life.

If someone close to you loses a parent, send him or her a note sharing a memory of that person. Include that friend in your next holiday celebration.

If a new family moves to your city, welcome them with invitations and tips on how to adapt to their new city or neighborhood. We all experience voids, low points, and the anxieties of being the new guy or girl on the block. Remember the ones who came through for you, and throw out some life preservers of your own. What goes around really does come around in the larger scheme of things.

8 Turn Off the Lite FM: Stay Forward-Focused, and Wrap Your Arms around Change

◼ Take Off the Blinders!

I always believe in having fresh eyes. Don't get so locked into your opinions and ambitions, or your ideas about yourself, that you can't hear or see what others are trying to tell you. Take off those blinders—now! As people get older, many seem to narrow their vision. They get hardened about their particular likes and dislikes.

They've made decisions and don't want to reconsider

them. This is how they're going to look and dress—in blue and gray, never red. They wear their eyeliner this way, and their lipstick that way, and that's it. They like this type of music, and they won't listen to any of that. They're committed to this political party, and they don't want to consider that one. They're all locked up.

How can you learn by shutting things out of your life: by wearing only black or white all the time, instead of having a mix-and-match wardrobe; or by refusing to be open to new opinions; or by hanging out with old college pals and never making a new friend? Where's the spirit, the discovery in this?

■ Don't Narrow the Range of What You Think about Yourself, Whether It's about Your Looks or How You Live Your Life.

When I go to my aerobics class, I love to hear new, loud and bracing and danceable music—whatever is new—and pop, even rap, that's what I want to work out to. Sometimes the other women in the class will groan and ask to hear the Beatles, or they'll want to work out to old disco tracks. That's so thirty years ago. Personally, I don't want to stick with a boomer soundtrack for the rest of my life.

Things were not necessarily better when you were young: they really weren't.

Keep yourself open to what's new. There's so much good new music out there, for example. Maybe Eminem is really talented and has a lot to say—no matter what he seems to be. He's an artist. If you just dismiss what's new out of hand, without investigating it or giving it a chance, you may be missing something.

◼ Don't Lock In to a Look or Style

While I've talked about the ways in which a solid routine can help you get through your average overcrowded day, I've learned that it is also crucial not to lock yourself in to a particular way of thinking or even a signature look. You can wind up like one of those petrified women on the society pages who look as though they haven't changed their hairstyles since the Reagan years.

I almost ended up a change-rejecter. If low-rise jeans had been around when I was young, I never would have worn them—too trendy. I wasn't that interested in keeping up with fashion, even though I enjoyed reading fashion magazines. And I couldn't imagine buying a new purse each season, or spending too much on one. My budget for a purse was something like ten dollars. If I were still "locked in" to that flower child look today that I had when I was young, I certainly would never have colored my hair or worn anything with sex appeal. It was a boyfriend who turned me on to the idea of making fashion work for me. He encouraged me to wear jeans that actually flattered my figure.

Finding a look that expresses who you are, or want to be, is part of growing as a person. It enables you to embrace change rather than hiding behind an appearance dictated by your mother or your best friend or by other social standards. But once you find that look, don't think it's the only one you can have for the next fifteen years.

You've got to keep your mind, and your appearance, open to change. Though you may strive not to be judged by what you look like, appearances do make a difference in this world, and adapting to the more superficial rules of the game can be a lot of fun.

Keep your look fresh and appropriate to the stage of life you're in. Nothing ages you more quickly than trying to look like someone you're not. Think about women like Christie Brinkley and Kim Basinger and Charlie's Angel Jaclyn Smith: these women are over fifty, and they look incredible. If they've had surgery, you can't tell; they look very natural. A lot of what keeps them looking young is that they've adapted their look to their age. They've evolved their hair and makeup and their fashion looks. They haven't allowed themselves to petrify.

If you're only thirty, for instance, and feel you're never going to change your hairstyle or your lipstick color or your ideas, you're not going to look like Christie Brinkley does at fifty. You'll look like Christie Brinkley's mother. You have to have the courage to change and evolve, no matter what your age.

When I get a haircut, I let the stylist tell me what he or she thinks about adjustments, maybe a new look or color. When one of the stylists at the salon I go to suggested that I add reddish tones a few years ago, I finally said, "Why not?" I liked it and went with it. Then more recently, the colorist I go to made me go even lighter by accident, but everyone liked that, too. So now I'm more of a redhead than the brunette I was all my life. It was an enhancing change, and I never would have done it on my own.

■ Turn Up That Stereo!

How you feel and how you look on the outside reflects your inner state. When you are open to new knowledge, ideas, and experiences, you are exercising the most important muscle in your body—your brain. Keeping your brain juiced will reflect on your face in a completely positive way. All the people I know who are fully engaged with life—working, creating, reading, planning, decision-making—look years younger than their numerical age.

Some people seem to think that their prime-time moment happens once in life, whether it's their wedding or their college graduation or the day they win their first big case. **Extend your prime-time moment until you're ninety! At least!** These days I work out five days a week and I push myself every time: I'm in better shape now than I was in my twenties. I can run farther and faster now. Keeping your muscles in shape fuels your energy level and helps sharpen the brain. If you don't use it, you will lose it. I believe that. It's worth it to keep both brain and body young.

You want to feel raring to make a difference in life whether you're twenty-five or sixty-five. I'm not a big believer in so-called age-appropriate behavior. You should always dance, for instance, no matter what your age. You want to feel attractive, that you have some measure of control over your life, that you're healthy and fit and have happy relationships. You want to be challenged and stimulated—not left out to pasture or locked in. Even with a crazy, busy life, you want to stay open to new ideas and to a sense of fun.

You can see the same patterns in the way people decorate their houses: they find a certain look and never change it. They are stuck in a certain era, with a certain style. They wouldn't think of repainting or redecorating, or selling the dishes they registered for when they got married at their next yard sale. Maybe they have no energy for new initiatives in their lives. If you can summon that energy, you'll find your life refreshed in ways you never dreamed were possible.

So how do you keep fresh eyes? Well, I read five newspapers every day and listen to the news. I go to lots of movies. I watch new TV shows. People are quick to whine about all the reality TV shows, but I find some of them fascinating. If you find yourself harrumphing that all the new shows are crap and that all reality TV shows are ridiculous, check yourself.

If I hadn't kept up with everything that's going on out there, I might not have seen the forest for the trees in terms of creating a new form of journalism that has taken the media by storm—the celebrity newsmagazine. Like it or not, celebrities are our contemporary pop culture's version of royalty. Readers and television and movie viewers want to see how their favorite stars live and dress and act.

So look in the mirror: are you a premature granny or a pop culture humbug? Take a breath and tune in to something new. Not all new music, art, and TV shows are inferior. Talent emerges all the time: keep an eye out for it. Clearly I don't think that things that are fun are necessarily silly or for airheads or not worth trying. I also don't believe that it's frivolous to spend some time and money on yourself. Enjoy a pedicure or a massage. Get highlights. Have a wardrobe of earrings.

Honor Your Inner Goofball

Who cares what other people think, if you're having a good time? Kids certainly help with this: they keep you young. They bring you new ideas and new ways of thinking. They force you to do new activities all the time, and you have to keep up with them in the sandbox and on the slide and all the rest of it. By the time you have teenagers, you'll have new connections through them to pop culture. Having children is regenerative for the parents, even in simple things such as finding a new story to read to your kids.

Never ever turn off your inner goofball. In fact, I think you should feed it. You want to recharge yours all the time. In some ways I'm truly geeky, and that's why I think some people don't get me.

Women today have the opportunity to have full lives and be multidimensional people, with different sides to their personality. You can be a major editorial director, but you can also be a goofball. Sometimes I still pack my lunch at home and take it into the office. You don't have to be one thing or another. You can be both. There is no reason to have a narrow view of yourself and your world and your life.

Have you ever noticed how little kids just burst with happiness, confidence, and crazy plans and dreams? They are goofy and silly and utterly lacking in self-consciousness. I'll never forget how each of my four children first started walking and talking: they didn't walk, they swaggered! They owned the world, bossy masters and mistresses of their own domains, convinced they could be anything they wanted to be when they grew up.

When do we stop swaggering and start second-guessing ourselves? **Maybe it's about time that you rediscovered your childhood confidence and became a born-again swaggerer.** A swagger can help you get back to the source of an energy you'll find refreshing and renewing. It puts you in touch with your younger, eager self, who was ready to take on all challenges, saw no limits to life's possibilities, and never thought of holding back because of an insecurity or inner voice of self-doubt.

To rediscover this self, give yourself some pep talks; pat yourself on the back from time to time. Make a conscious and active decision to throw away the knives you've been using on yourself. Focus on what you're good at—everyone is good at something—and impress others with that skill. If you're a good cook, invite friends over to dinner to share the fruits of your labors. Let others see your strengths.

It's important, too, to make new friends who may be a bit younger than you, especially if you don't have children to connect you to the enthusiasms shared by members of their generation. Younger friends can help you keep a fresh outlook and avoid locking in to a particular style or mode of living.

In addition, it's important to have connectors in your life, people who naturally connect with others, whether they are younger than you or not. Connectors, like friends in the next generation, can help you stay abreast of the latest developments in pop culture, fashion, and the news of the day.

A friend who is a great connector encourages you to try that new restaurant or even that new lipstick color, or drags you out to dinner to meet someone new he or she knows you'd like. I can get so immersed in work that I become a kind of shut-in. If you don't have connectors in your life, you need to go and find some—at the gym, through a book discussion group, or even online.

Connectors get their energy from connecting, so let them do what they enjoy and do best. Often they turn connecting into their work, in career placement or public relations. Their cell phones ring constantly; they have a million friends. If you are still lacking some of the elements of a joyfully full life, developing new friendships with connectors can widen your personal and professional circle in truly enriching ways.

The Full Life, at Any Age

Every person I know who is hungrily alive and productive over sixty-five is still passionately at work: Oleg Cassini, the designer; Leonard Lauder, chairman of Estée Lauder; David Brown, the producer; Helen Gurley Brown, the editor; Frank Bennack Jr., chairman of the executive committee at Hearst. And look at Viacom's CEO and chairman of the board, Sumner Redstone: he's in his eighties. Don Hewitt, the former executive producer of *60 Minutes* was well into his eighties before he stopped running the show on a daily basis. In the *New York Times* I read an interview with a man who is 101 and still goes to the office three or four days a week: he was a partner in a big investment company.

What's the secret to a long life? the reporter asked.

"You just keep moving," he replied. "You keep living and doing."

He walks everywhere; he stays active and denies himself little because of his age. It's a mental attitude. He wants to live his life to the fullest, for the longest time that he can.

Some people exude a contagious vitality that I'd like to emulate as I age. I interviewed Oleg Cassini twenty years ago for the *Toronto Star,* when he was seventy-one. He'd been Jackie Kennedy's wardrobe designer when she was in the White House. I was utterly taken with his charisma and vitality. I'd never met a seventy-one-year-old man who was so vital and sexy—so *not old.* In the intervening years, I'd had no further contact with him.

He's now ninety-one. Recently he won an award, and I just called him out of the blue for a lunch date. We talked about how busy he is, at ninety-one. He is full of life. He works every day and is an avid athlete. When I asked him if he still played tennis and rode horses, he replied, "I do these things, but I don't think of them as 'still.' I just do them."

Part of his good health is no doubt genetic. He's also never been a big drinker and never smoked. He's always been athletic and robust, he told me. He was in the Navy with John Kennedy in World War II. He told me he plans to work for another twelve years. And after that, he'll make another twelve-year plan: the focus is always forward, despite the fact that he's losing many of his peers. So he makes new, younger friends as well.

▇ Push the Edge of the Envelope!

This is how I want to be. This is the full life, saying yes to much too much—to new people and experiences even at age ninety-one, to keeping active and not spending much time looking backward or regretting what wasn't. **Doing— being involved—is what leads you to happiness.** Ultimately what we all want is a long and full life. Every day Oleg Cassini is involved in something new; he's not sitting around clipping old reports for his scrapbook. I just don't believe that indulgent reflection is a good thing for achieving happiness: active engagement in encountering new ideas and meeting new people is key. His philosophy of life matches mine, despite our age difference.

Some people seem to feel that it requires too much work, or too great an expenditure of energy, to keep up with everything new in the world. I think the opposite is true: the more you stay locked in to your old ways, the harder it will be to change them. If you take yourself out of the game, it's over.

I can't emphasize enough how important it is to take risks, at every stage of your life. I've been the editor of a teen publication, of a fashion magazine, of a women's service magazine, and of a celebrity newsweekly. Now I'm an editorial director of a number of different publications. I haven't stagnated; I've been able to break out of a narrow slot. Look for opportunities to expand the range of what you do and how you think. Push yourself to stretch. If you reach one goal, set another, and take pleasure out of going for it.

■ Don't Make De-Stressing Your Life a Goal

I sometimes think that too much has been made of stress as a bad thing in life. We've become obsessed with the idea that we now lead more stressful lives than anyone ever did before. But consider this: there is nothing experienced by most middle-class people today that compares to what much of humankind has gone through on a daily basis. Most middle-class Americans control their lives to some degree; they've made choices about how they want to live. What's most stressful is having no control at all. OK. So you have a demanding boss, and work that needs to be done, and a child who has to get to his or her playdate. These aren't the kind of stresses so many people in the history of the world have had to endure: fear of death or plague, of not having enough to eat, of war and persecution. These were—and are—*real* stresses.

It is not stressful to wonder when you can fit in your hairdressing appointment or if you'll be late for your workout. These are luxuries. Real stresses that we truly face today are the biggies: cheating lovers, personal and family illness, divorce—your own, or your parent or child's— demeaning or cruel bosses, financial setbacks, job losses, addictions, depressions—or being a hurricane victim. These are all serious problems and terribly, awfully stressful. They do not bring on good stress, and they require serious help and attention. I'm just saying that you need to keep perspective and not identify your messy house and inability to have a "perfect" Martha Stewart–looking life as a reason to put yourself under serious strain.

Even many real stresses can be good for you in some way, because they force you to prioritize and to eliminate things that are not essential. And like envy, normal stress can be used as a motivator. **I would much rather suffer from normal stress than die of boredom.**

When your mind isn't stimulated for long periods of time, it atrophies. We've all heard those stories of people who retire to play golf and are dead a year later. They don't surprise me.

We weren't meant to live without the stimulus of striving. Though the "hunt-gather-survive" ethos is no longer relevant today, it is still essential for us to be actively engaged in work, to be mentally and physically alive in our endeavors.

Jump-Start Your Own Life

You don't want to wait for a tragedy or a downturn in your life to help jump-start you—though sometimes these awful and tearful moments are defining points that push you to make your life more meaningful. That's what happened to Stephanie Greenfield, who owns the highly successful Scoop women's specialty boutiques in Manhattan and elsewhere. Her best friend growing up was Allie Gertz, a smart, brave, New York City girl who died at age twenty-one from AIDs, contracted during a one-night stand. It happened early in the epidemic, when there weren't many treatments available.

Her death was heartbreaking: Allie so much wanted to live, to have a career and a relationship and kids. When Stephanie lost her best friend, it gave her the kick to get her own business going, making her realize that this is not a dress rehearsal: you've got to make use of your life. You can't just sit. You have to do, in order to make your dreams a reality.

Too often women get comfortable, or they're afraid, and they don't take living to the next level. They get into a rut of going to work—they don't love the job, but it's OK—making enough money, and then going to meet their girl-friends at a bar, often the same bar every time. They hang out and then get takeout to eat at home and watch TV. The next day they start the same routine all over again.

▮ Just OK Is Never Enough

This life is not terrible; it's OK. But it's *just* OK. These women are not stretching, in terms of career or relation-ships. They're in a rut. And a lot of them are waiting for the White Knight to come along and lift them out of the rut. The truth is that **a life that's just OK is *not* OK.**

In a life like this, you're letting your time tick-tock away. **Don't let "somewhat acceptable" be enough for you.** Because if you do that, you can wind up bitter, asking your-self, "Well, why is so-and-so doing so much better? Why do they have a husband? Why did they get a promotion?"

If you don't get passionate about what you're doing in the different areas of your life—and you don't make that passion drive you to achieve more at work, or get more creative, or find new friends, or find a man, or a new interest, any of the things that can make your life more interesting and fulfilling—if you don't do that, after a while you will get depressed or bitter, two responses that will paralyze, not motivate you.

You have to think of life as a train that is always moving forward. It will stop at a few stations for a few minutes, and if you're not on it yet, you have an opportunity to jump on board. But if you don't, the train will pull out and just keep going.

I have a friend, a valued staff photographer at a major newspaper, who didn't marry until she was almost forty. Although barely five feet tall and not a size two, she always looked great. So did the apartment she put together as a single woman, not waiting for a man to help her put down roots. She loved to decorate. One day while visiting her and admiring an antique dresser she had added to the living room, I asked her, "How did you afford it?"

I'll always remember her answer: "It's so hard to find just the right thing that when I see it in a store or at auction, I buy it and worry about how to pay for it later. Somehow I manage."

She was right. While I would never endorse careless spending or racking up credit card debt, sometimes you need to take chances, and you need to take them now. If a certain purchase or career move or exotic trip is absolutely the right thing for you, don't deprive yourself. And even more importantly, don't drive yourself crazy with guilt after you've gone and made your move.

Do what needs to be done, and relish both the risk and the reward.

If you look at it this way, you'll see that **leaping into the unknown is in fact less risky than accepting the status quo.** You have no choice but to drive yourself forward. Whether it's a new hair color or a new lifestyle or a new way of thinking about yourself and your situation, you need to take that first step, because at a certain point in your life—trust me—**what's merely comfortable will turn stagnant.** Make your moves before you wake up one day and find yourself in this position.

If you find that you've lost your passion, the challenge is to boot yourself back up. **Don't quit on life and wind up taking fallback positions because they seem easier.** Don't say, "Well, I'm not madly in love with this man, but maybe he'll do." Or "My job isn't what I hoped for, so maybe I'll just stay home with the kids and see what happens." Or "I think I'll quit the rat race and live in a little cabin somewhere."

People who think this way almost seem to be envisioning themselves as characters in a movie they've yet to be cast in, people like the leads in Albert Brooks's *Lost in America*, a New York executive and his wife who sell everything to create a "nest egg" then set out in a trailer to find a new life. They blow the nest egg and end up flipping hamburgers. In the end, they zoom back to New York and beg for their old jobs back.

You can change your life, but you can't retire from it. You can't deny the power and energy of your personality: if you've been a hard-driving, competitive person with an ultra-full life, I don't think you can successfully flip-flop to a laid-back, "simple" life. You may not go nuts, but you certainly could go into a major depression, because you aren't operating at the speed that comes most naturally to you. So, choose to opt up, not out. Imagine your best scenario of what you want to do and take the steps necessary to begin to go for it. If you feel overwhelmed with the combo of both work and family, try to change your way of looking at your situation. Look at its positives: the richness that your too-full, all-too-much life provides. And maybe, in order to have more control, more power, and yes, more money, you need to take yourself to the next level. *That* will actually de-stress your life somewhat.

If things aren't going your way, you have to reorder your stand. There's no denying that things can get difficult at times. You can be stuck with a bad boss or a situation with too much politics in the company, or your whole industry can go into decline. But I think it's important not to sour on trying to have that full life. I know women who quit their jobs when they had kids; then when the kids get into high school, and the mothers are ready to get back into things, they don't know how. It's hard to get back in when you've been on the sidelines for so long. In fact the time you spend raising kids—especially if you only have one or two—is a relatively short span in a long life.

You need to ask yourself not how you can abandon everything, but how you can parlay the passion that motivates you most strongly into a part of your everyday life. This may mean making not a complete right- or left-hand turn but maybe taking the Y, the fork in the road. Whether by finding a new job or a hobby, you want to wind up spending your daytime hours doing what your really *like* to do.

The life of much too much is one that opens all paths and leaves you with the freedom to be the person you were born to be, in every way.

The too full life is never complete; it is always open to further evolution. It is never a done deal, with doors closed off or options shut down. The person with the full life never stops growing. He or she keeps developing new interests and abilities and looking for new ways to connect with others and cultivate new depths of feeling or a more complex and interesting inner life.

The too-full life of much too much is never routine or

settled. There may be routines in it, but they are the means to an end.

Once having a too-full life becomes a way of being—a habit, if you will—you have prepared yourself for your later years. "Bored" or "cynical" will never describe you. You won't be spending your senior years in a retirement community because you will never retire. There will always be possibilities for new knowledge and experience, for reading, for research that needs to be done.

Don't edit yourself or hold yourself back from acting on a solid intuition or a good idea. Give it a shot. Relish how it makes you feel. Psych yourself up to fight the battles that are important to you. Never back down from a challenge or an opportunity because someone says to you, "That is just too much," whether it's about having another child, taking on a bigger job, or scaling a mountaintop.

Much too much is just right. It is exactly what you want and need, to be fully alive, at every moment of your life.

Index

Advertising Age, 180

affirmative action program, 40–41, 42

aging, 195-201

Allure, 26, 114

American Media, 2–3, 64, 182

Amnesty International Award, 146, 148

apologizing, 166–67

appearance, 26, 31, 60–61, 62–63, 109, 132–34, 197–99

appreciation, showing, 158, 166

Arrington, Chris, 34

attention: getting, 20–21, 51–53, 62, 158–59

available, keeping yourself, 21–25

bad-mouthing, 68, 73, 76–78, 164

Bahrenburg, Claeys, 55–56

Bassett, Doug, 10

beauty: and getting ahead, 41–44

Beckham, David, 112

being noticed, 20–21, 51–53, 73, 158–59

beliefs, 145–48

Bennack, Frank Jr., 204

biological clock, 97–102

"black holes," 72

blogging, negative, 76–78

bosses/employers: and dos and don'ts, 71–81; loyalty to, 74, 75, 77, 163, 172, 173, 174. *See also specific person or organization*

Brown, David, 1–2, 3, 204

Brown, Helen Gurley, 20, 42, 48, 55, 204

careers: derailers of, 76–78; as giving life, 84; giving up, 117–18; and love/marriage, 84–85, 89–90; and motherhood, 104–5, 110–14; as passions, 171; rewards of building, 88; second, 82; sidelining, 85–88. *See also* jobs

Carey, Mariah, 170

Cassini, Oleg, 204, 205, 206

catastrophizing, 190–91

celebrities, 152–53, 156

celebrity journalism, 148–53, 156–57, 201

Celebrity Living, 20, 157

change: openness to, 195–214; and sticking to your mission, 141–67

children: as goofballs, 202; having, 96–102; as regenerative for parents, 201; staying home with, 85–88; traveling/vacations with, 111–12, 128–29. *See also* family; motherhood; parenting; pregnancy; working mothers

Clinton, Bill, 147, 148

215

Clinton, Hillary, 42, 114
cold calls, 59, 176
commitment, 49, 69, 89–90, 93–94,
    104–5, 126, 164
compartmentalization, 190–91
complaining, 71–72, 76–79
Condé Nast, 36, 50, 111, 170, 173,
    175, 177. *See also specific*
    magazine
confidence, 17, 33, 41–44, 60,
    61–62, 66, 85, 96, 159, 160, 202
connections, making, 32–34, 49,
    55–56, 57, 176
connectors, 203–4
contingencies, 63, 88, 131–37
control issues, 139–40
Cosmopolitan: and Brown-Fuller
    relationship, 48, 55; and Fuller as
    Editor of the Year, 180; and Fuller
    as mother, 113; Fuller as pregnant
    while at, 110; Fuller hired by, 48;
    Fuller leaves, 163; Fuller's
    accomplishments at, 2; and Fuller's
    firing from *Glamour*, 172; and
    Fuller's *Glamour* offer, 173; Fuller's
    mission at, 145; Fuller's pregnancy
    while at, 106; Hearst as owner of,
    172; as opportunity for Fuller, 49;
    rivals of, 173; and Robertson-
    Fuller relationship, 49; and sticking
    to your mission, 145, 163
crisis. *See* disasters/crisis
criticism: constructive, 161–62; and
    sticking to your mission, 141–67
Crow, Elizabeth, 33–34, 36
Curry, Ann, 41

"dark side," 38–40
defensiveness, 162
deficits, 29–31
denial, 1–12
disasters/crisis: acting quickly and
    decisively in, 185–89; as character-
    defining moments, 183; fighting
    your way back from, 176–82; and
    Fuller's firing from *Glamour*, 169,

170–76, 183, 187, 189, 192; help
    during, 192–93; and jump-starting
    your own life, 208–9; keeping
    moving after, 183–85; personal,
    78–79, 183–89; positive aspects
    of, 180; and repression, 190–91
divorce, 86, 87–88, 95
doing your best, 4, 48–51, 80–81,
    114, 116–17, 145
Dolce, Joe, 3, 72, 150–51
double standard, 112–14, 187
dreams: importance of, 44–45; and
    jump-starting your own life, 209;
    realizing your, 47–82. *See also*
    goals

Editor of the Year, 180
Elle, 29, 155
employers. *See* bosses/employers;
    specific person or organization
energy, 61, 104–5, 126, 200, 202,
    203, 206, 212
enthusiasm, 16, 61, 67, 104
envy, 44–45
Esquire, 51–52

facts: facing, 1–3, 9; foot-in-the-door,
    58–59
failure, 169–76, 181
family: and coming back from
    disasters, 171; and making
    arrangements that work for you,
    110–12; and managing an
    unbalanced life, 122–23, 125–26;
    "perfect time" for starting, 96–97;
    putting off having, 98–102. *See*
    also children
fashion, 18–19, 20–29, 31, 48–49,
    154–55, 197–99. *See also specific*
    magazine
fear, 3, 7–9, 12, 90
first impressions, 91–92
fixation, inner, 191–92
Flare, 25–31, 32, 34, 49, 50, 52, 57,
    61, 109, 142
flexibility, 122–23

following the pack, 38–40
foot-in-the-door facts, 58–59
Ford, Eileen, 15
Ford, Katie, 15
Ford, Lacey, 15
Four Seasons restaurant (New York City), 133–34, 180
Fuller, Bonnie: accomplishments of, 2–3, 37, 180; career goals of, 9; childhood and youth of, 13–15, 35, 86–87, 143; college years of, 9–10, 66; early New York years of, 21–25, 30, 32–36; early professional career of, 15–19, 20–29, 30, 32–36, 48–49; as Editor of the Year, 180; family background of, 85–88; law school years of, 15–16, 17; salary of, 181–82
Fuller, Leilah, 101, 102–3, 121, 128, 183–87, 189, 190, 191, 192
Fuller, Michael: first impression of, 92; and Fuller's career commitments, 90; Fuller's engagement to, 25; Fuller's relationship with, 91, 93–94; and Fuller's *Us Weekly* job offer, 179; and having children, 96, 101; and Leilah's illness, 184, 185–86, 187–88; and managing an unbalanced life, 121, 122, 123, 125, 126, 128, 129, 138–40; and Robertson-Fuller relationship, 50; and ultimatums, 93–94
Fuller, Noah, 96–97, 100, 103, 109, 121, 123, 128
Fuller, Sasha, 100, 102, 103, 114, 121, 171, 174
Fuller, Sofia, 102, 121, 123, 171, 183, 188, 189

Garner, Jennifer, 37–38
Gertz, Allie, 208–9
getting ahead, 41–44, 74
getting stuck, 81
Glamour: advertising sales at, 172; awards for, 146, 148; circulation of, 2, 155; as Condé Nast magazine, 26; Fuller as a mother while at, 114; Fuller as pregnant while at, 110, 114; Fuller joins, 163; Fuller's accomplishments at, 2; and Fuller's beliefs, 145–48; as Fuller's favorite as teenager, 15; Fuller's firing from, 2, 169, 170–76, 183, 187, 189, 192; Fuller's salary at, 181–82; Fuller's vision for, 145–48, 155; rivals of, 29, 173; Robertson at, 49; and sticking to your mission, 145–48, 155, 163; Whitney as editor of, 33, 172–73; and women's rights, 146–48; Zeta-Jones's covers on, 174–76
goals, 144, 158, 160. *See also* dreams
goofball: inner, 201–4
Google, 11
Gordon, Ruth, 1, 2
Greenfield, Stephanie, 208–9
grudges, 24, 138
Gruner & Jahr, 33–34
guilt, 84, 113, 117, 119–22, 139, 211

handshakes, 63–64
Haobsh, Nadine, 77
hard work, 29, 54, 66, 69, 144–45
Harper's Bazaar, 29, 155, 172, 173
Hearst Publications, 37, 55–56, 172, 173
help, 42, 192–93
Hess, Jane, 25, 51–52, 92
Hilfiger, Tommy, 55, 56
Hinman, Veronica, 177–78
hope, 189
humor, sense of, 21, 61, 65, 127

"I can't do it," 10
ignoring the odds, 47–82
In Style, 61, 155
independence, 85–88
initiative, 16
inner voices, 159, 160, 186, 202
instincts, 37–40, 123, 161, 214
interviews: dressing for, 19; during

pregnancy, 104; exit, 164; follow-up to, 69–71; getting, 56–59; nailing the, 63–69; preparing for, 59–63; waiting for, 68
introductory letters, 58
Ivy League, 65–66

jobs: acceptance of offers of, 70–71; and admitting mistakes, 165–67; changing, 81; dead-end, 51; dos and don'ts on, 71–82; gofer, 48; leaving, 163–64; and motherhood, 112–14; pregnancy on, 105–9; returning to, 165–66; as a right not a privilege, 71–72; searching for, 32–36, 176–79, 186; small, 51–52; turning down, 71. *See also* careers
journalism: celebrity, 148–53, 156–57, 201; death of serious, 150
just OK, 209–14

keeping options open, 32–33

Leno, Mavis, 146
life: being fully engaged with, 199–200, 204–6; changing your, 212; too-full, 213–14
life supplies: and managing an unbalanced life, 131–37
listening, 79–80
Living Room, 177
losing, 40–41, 42, 43, 69–70, 169–76, 181
love/marriage: and careers, 84–85, 89–90; and control issues, 139–40; finding, 83–114; and first impressions, 91–92; and independence, 85–88; and managing an unbalanced life, 137–40; and right man, 88–90; and romance, 137–40; and ultimatums, 93–96; unconditional, 90–92
loving: of inner self, 42
loyalty, 74, 75, 77, 163, 172, 173, 174
lying, 69

Mademoiselle, 15, 32–33, 36, 37
make-things-happen mind-set, 3–5
malcontents, 72–73
Marie Claire: and "dark side," 39–40; and Fuller at fashion shows, 31; Fuller hired by, 37, 55; Fuller leaves, 49; Fuller's accomplishments at, 2; and Fuller's appearance, 31; and Fuller's firing from *Glamour,* 172; Fuller's interview with, 61; Fuller's vision for, 38, 39–40, 154; Hearst as owner of, 37, 172; launching of American edition of, 37, 56; and opportunities for Fuller, 49; and pregnancy in workplace, 104; readers of, 154; and Robertson-Fuller relationship, 49
Maurer, Gil, 37, 55–56, 65
McHugh, Clare, 61, 104
Meredith Publishing, 177
mission: and admitting mistakes, 165–67; and celebrity journalism, 148–53; and costs of decisions, 163; and criticism, 158, 159–62; and doing what you believe in, 145–48; and leaving jobs, 163–64; and perfection, 153–57; sticking to your, 141–67; and taking responsibility, 143–44; and taking the rap, 143–45; and trying, 148–51
mistakes: admitting, 165–67
models/modeling agencies, 30, 38, 153
money, 84, 85–86, 118
morale, 71–72, 73
motherhood, 212–13. *See also* pregnancy; working mothers
"must have" lists, 88–89, 90
Myers, Mike, 13

naysayers, 5–7, 159. *See also* criticism
needy workers, 78–79
negatives: blogging, 76–78; flattening of, 31; and having full life, 88–89; and interviews, 68; and job dos

and don'ts, 73, 76–78; and loving
inner loser, 40–41, 42, 43; and
sticking to your mission, 159–61;
and turning negatives into
positives, 13–45. See also bad-
mouthing; criticism
networking. See connections, making
New York Post, 128, 173
New York Times, 113, 171, 204
New Yorker, 150
Newhouse, Si, 170
Noyes, Nicole, 101

obsessions, 116
openness: to change, 195–214; to
happy accidents, 17–19; and
love/marriage, 91–92; to
opportunities, 36–37, 54; and
sticking to your mission, 161
opportunities, 36–37, 48–51, 54
Ottawa Citizen newspaper, 16, 17, 18,
19
overachievers, 16–17

Page, Larry, 11
parenting, 121–22, 201. See also
motherhood; working mothers
passions: careers as, 171; and changing
your life, 210, 213; and coming
back from disasters, 171;
discovering, 84; finding your,
47–82; hobbies as, 82; and letting
it find you, 49
Pecker, David, 182
People, 148, 149, 156, 157, 181
perfection, 120–21, 123, 127, 153–57
Perry Ellis clothing company, 53–54
persistence, 23, 26, 28, 34, 59, 70
personality, 41–44, 212
photographers, 29–30, 38
politeness, 60, 64
popularity: and sticking to your
mission, 141–67
positives: and being positive, 68; and
coming back from disasters, 170,
180; and having a full life, 88–89;

and job dos and don'ts, 71–72;
and managing an unbalanced life,
123; and saving positive energy for
right employers, 104–5; turning
negatives into, 13–45
power, 41–44, 108–9
praise, 158
pregnancy, 104, 105–9
prime-time moments, 199–200
priorities, 117–20, 208
problems. See disasters/crisis
proof of worthiness, 58–59
pushing yourself forward, 56–57

rejection, 69–70. See also losing
repression: good side of, 190–91
Rifkinson, Stephanie, 183
risk taking, 206, 211
Roberts, Julia, 181
Robertson, Donald, 39–40, 49–51,
66, 92, 153
romance, 137–40
Rose, Vicci, 133
routines, 130–31, 171, 176–77, 189,
209, 213–14
Rubenstein, Atoosa, 43

sacrifices, 117–18
Scott, Donna, 25
self: affirmative action program for,
40–41; hidden resources within,
100; loving inner, 42; re-creating,
177–78
self-criticism, 5–7
self-esteem, 17
self-image, 196–97, 202
self-obsession, 4
Seventeen, 3, 14–15, 22, 35, 43, 77
Sgroi, Barbara, 26, 27, 28
Short, Martin, 13
Shriftman, Lara, 53–54
Star: and "black holes," 72; celebrity
cooperation for contents of, 176;
and celebrity journalism, 149,
150–53; circulation of, 156; as
escape magazine, 151; focus groups

at, 157; format of, 157; Fuller joins, 182; Fuller's accomplishments at, 2–3; and Fuller's management of unbalanced life, 124; Fuller's vision for, 150–53; and pushing yourself forward, 57; reputation of, 150–51; revitalization of, 182; rivals of, 182; spin-off of, 157; and sticking to your mission, 156–57; Walsh at, 165
stress, 207–8, 212
superficiality, 25–29

taking the rap, 143–45
13 Going on 30 (film), 37–38
Toronto Life, 51–52
Toronto Star newspaper, 15, 16, 17, 18–19, 20–21, 25, 52, 205
travel/vacations, 111–12, 128–29, 139
Truman, James, 175
trust, 122, 140, 174
trying: keeping on, 148–51

ultimatums, 93–96
unbalanced life: and guilt, 117, 119–21, 139; and life supplies, 131–37; managing your, 115–40; and no such thing as balance, 115–16; and romance, 137–40; and routines, 130–31; short cuts for, 123–28
University of Toronto, 9, 66
Us Weekly: and celebrity journalism, 148–50, 176; circulation of, 156, 180; columns in, 156; Fuller offered job at, 179–80; Fuller's accomplishments at, 2, 3; Fuller's early months at, 180–81, 186; and Fuller's management of unbalanced life, 133–34; Fuller's salary at, 181–82; Fuller's vision for, 156, 181; rivals of, 181, 182; and sticking to your mission, 156; Walsh at, 165

vacations. *See* travel/vacations
Vardolos, Nia, 43
Vogue, 26, 29, 155, 175–76
voice mail messages, 58

Wallin, Pamela, 84
Walsh, Darren, 165
Weiner, Michael, 184, 186
Wells, Linda, 114
Wenner, Jann, 179, 180, 181, 182
"what ifs," 120
Whitney, Ruth, 33, 172–73
"Why Not?" club, 8–12
Wintour, Anna, 132, 175–76
women's rights, 146–48
Women's Wear Daily, 22–24, 32, 53–54, 55
"won't do" lists, 88–89
work ethic, 48–51. *See also* doing your best; hard work
working mothers: and careers, 104–5, 110–14; and double standard, 112–14; and giving up careers, 117–18; priorities and sacrifices of, 117–20; and right time for motherhood, 96–97; unbalanced life of, 115–40. *See also* motherhood

Yahoo, 11
Young Miss (*YM*): and being noticed, 52–53; Bertelsmann as owner of, 36; circulation of, 35; columns in, 153–54; focus groups for, 52–53, 106–7, 153–54; Fuller offered job at, 34; Fuller's accomplishments at, 2, 3, 37; Fuller's vision for, 35–36, 38, 39, 40, 49–51, 153–54; and opportunities for Fuller, 49; and pushing yourself forward, 57; rivals of, 3, 35; and Robertson-Fuller relationship, 49–51

Zeta-Jones, Catherine, 174–76

about the author

Bonnie Fuller has led America's most popular magazines, including *Glamour, Cosmopolitan, Us Weekly,* and *Star,* to record successes. Twice a winner of *Advertising Age*'s prestigious Editor of the Year Award, Bonnie Fuller is the editorial director at American Media, where she oversees a galaxy of magazines, including America's number-one celebrity newsweekly, *Star.* She lives in New York with her husband and four children.